A History of Sweets in 50 Wrappers

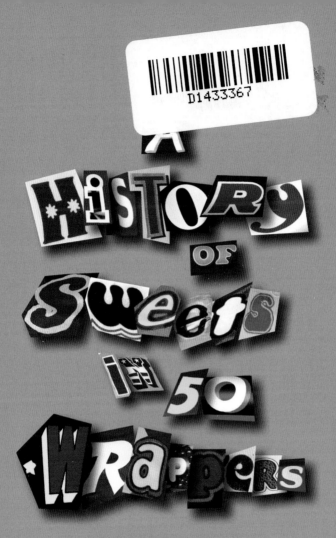

STEVE BERRY & PHIL NORMAN

THE
FRIDAY
PROJECT

Image cedits

Confectionery collections: Lucy Bernstein, John Estlea
(http://bit.ly/lyonsmaid), Dan Goodsell, Darren Wallington
(http://bit.ly/70sCrispPackets).

Comic pages: Combom, Steve Hearn, Alistair McGown.

Badges: Frank Setchfield (http://www.badgecollectorscircle.co.uk).

First published in Great Britain in 2014 by
The Friday Project
An imprint of HarperCollinsPublishers
77–85 Fulham Palace Road
London W6 8JB
www.harpercollins.co.uk

Some of the content of this book originally appeared in *The Great British
Tuck Shop*, published by The Friday Project in 2012

Copyright © Steve Berry and Phil Norman 2014

1

A catalogue record for this book is available from the British Library

ISBN 9780007575480

Original design and layout by Concrete Armchair
Additional design work by Clarissa San Pedro and Luana Gobbo
Illustrations by Jumping Bean Bag Ltd
Printed and bound in China

Three favourite Spangles—
a taste of the good old days!

Old English...Acid Drop...Barley Sugar...
...ee favourites from the Spangles range of nine big-value packs. **Always in flavour, always good value.**

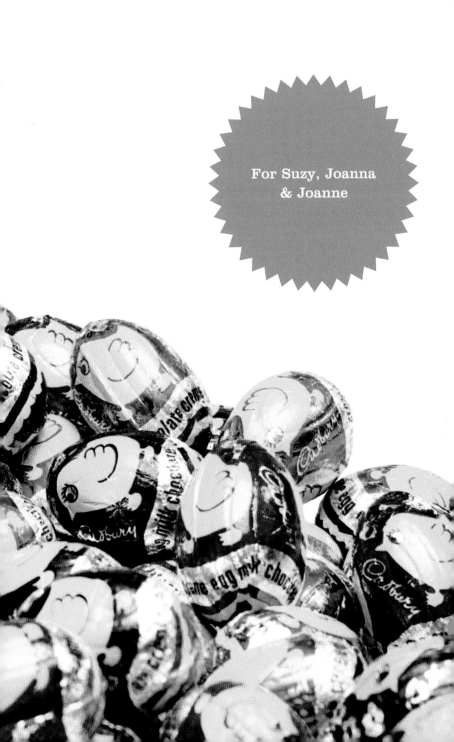

For Suzy, Joanna
& Joanne

Contents

THE KIDS IN YOUR SHOP ARE GOING TO BE ASKING FOR IT.

Manufactured by:
A. McCowan & Sons Ltd.,
Stenhousemuir,
Stirlingshire.

They've heard all about Wham on the radio, it's being backed by our biggest ever promotional spend.

The fruity, chewy, space age bar that sizzles with sherbet and only costs 10p.

And when they find out they can get a free space poster with Wham Bars there'll be no holding them back.

So order your supplies at your usual wholesalers or cash and carry now – **and get 20 pence off your first outer with the coupon below.**

And let them have it.

A wholesaler's handling fee of 1p per coupon will be paid.

INTRODUCTION

For anyone of a certain age, memories of childhood are irrevocably connected to the stomach. The sweet shop was a great leveller. Everyone shopped there, from the Walter Softies to the Bully Beefs (although the bullies would probably steal the softies' sweets, too). If you were a Milky Bar kid, a Flake girl or one of Fry's Five Boys, it's likely that the very first purchase you made with your very own money was something to eat.

There are two acknowledged golden ages of British confectionery. The first came in the 1920s and 1930s when, despite the Depression, the big sweet makers consolidated their brands and expanded nationwide. The second came in the 1970s and 1980s when, despite the Depression, the big names of sweets let their development departments go (fruit and) nuts, shunting out celebrity-endorsed chocolate bars and cartoon-wrapped nougat delights on a weekly basis.

Manufacturing went Technicolor, all the better to catch the wavering eye and stick in the mind for years to come. Sweet shops, until then like antique shops – arthritic, grey and fusty, trapping sunbeams in dust and quietly ossifying – were transformed into glittering Aladdin's caves, crammed to the rafters with individually wrapped sugared treasures.

Somewhere between decimalisation and globalisation, creative confectionery enjoyed its most fertile period – an auspicious era that began with the last manned moon mission and ended as the first Sky channels beamed into unsuspecting British homes. That journey to the corner shop took on the nature of a pilgrimage for many a child, with a salivating smile and a skipping heartbeat. Inside, a fantastic cornucopia of riches. Some items had a past longer than the shopkeeper himself. Others would go on to outlive him. While many, with hindsight, would never see the year out.

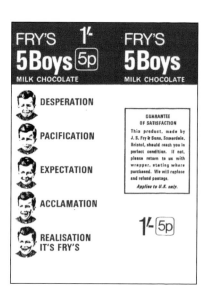

Opposite: 'Oh, pish, tush and a cheap laugh during a slow edition of *Oh! It's Fry's Five Boys* (1902).

Below: Fings ain't what they used to be (1981), not least for the racist packaging of Trebor's Black Jacks (1920).

3

None of this mattered to your prospective sweet purchaser, gloriously transfixed as they were in the moment, surveying the ranks of stock. Iconic Mars bars sitting next to the doomed likes of the Cadbury's Alamo. The Fruit Salad chew, old as the Book of Genesis, shared shelf space with Trebor's Fings, Rowntree's Junglies and other sugary mayflies. In the disinterested eyes of the proprietor, all products, as long as someone bought them, were equal. No preferential treatment here. You had to choose wisely, as funds were limited. Governmental sweet rationing may have ended in 1953, but the economic and parental varieties still held sway.

Many products came and went – mere footnotes in their manufacturers' inventories – but that doesn't mean they weren't coveted, adored, consumed with a passion and, just like old friends, noisily revisited a few hours later on the waste ground behind the prefabs. Fortunately a lot of them tasted the same coming up as going down.

The marketing men inevitably loom large in this tale, coupling childlike imagination with ruthless raiding of money boxes to create a world of hedonistic abandon, populated by models, mascots and maniacal showbiz personalities all merrily hooked on the product – whatever it may be – and keen to let the whole world know. Often in full song.

For better or worse, their efforts made a generation what it is, and what follows is, as much as anything else, an account of how they focus-grouped our Five Centres.

Those big companies can't help but tinker with their winning brands, all in the name of progress. Recipes are changed, formulas are tweaked, and – most heinously of all – the packaging is modernised. Do not despair. Despite the disappearance of some cherished childhood chocolate bars, many sweets, crisps, snacks and pop are still available if you look hard enough. Only the artificial colours and preservatives have been jettisoned, in favour of 'all natural' ingredients.

Don't believe those people who wax lyrical about the good old days of gobstoppers the size of your head, either. No, those Creme Eggs haven't got smaller. Your hands have got bigger. In fact, with very few exceptions, the tuck shop fare of youth is served in heftier portions than ever before, as the waddling, wobbling outlines of twenty-first-century obesity crises serve to illustrate.

So here it is, then, your very own unnatural preservative of the best of the Great British sweet shop. Go ahead, dive in – but don't spoil your tea, now.

50

WRAPPERS

*AERO

F or all the Wonka-esque mystique affected by chocolate makers, most confectionery innovations amount to 'let's bung this on top of this, stick some chocolate on it'. The invention of the Aero, however, really did involve science. Rowntree's technicians frothed up some liquid chocolate with a whisk, poured it into moulds and

Opposite: 'Unforgettabubble, that's what you are. Unforgettabubble, milk chocolate bar.' A line of old King Cole for Rowntree's Aero (1935).

7

then – the clever bit – reduced the surrounding air pressure drastically so the tiny bubbles of froth swelled up to a decent size. Then it was a matter of passing the moulds through ice-cold water to set, covering the result with a layer of solid chocolate, and the job was done.

It caused a sensation when it came out, albeit one helpfully whipped up by Rowntree themselves. The exciting new texture, they claimed, 'stimulates the enzyme glands' – a bit of shameless quackery they were soon forced to take back. Initially great sales began to tail off, in part due to an assortment of rivals appearing on the scene with undue haste, in particular Fry's two tryouts, the Ripple and the All-Chocolate Crunchie. Add to that a disputed patent, and things got panicky at Rowntree headquarters. Fruit and nut and whole nut variants were hurriedly bunged out to support the ailing novelty. Sales levelled off after a while, and the Aero, while no longer a craze, remained steady-as-she-goes.

They couldn't resist mucking about, though. An Aero Wafer introduced in 1950 didn't hang about too long, but in '59 the bright idea of changing the aerated centre from chocolate to peppermint gave the bar a new lease of life, and with orange and coffee centres arriving over the next couple of years, a nice little family was built up that would tick

over happily for decades, with just a new campaign based around the word 'bubbles' knocked out every few years. Oh, and a short-lived lime variant in 1971.

Then, cometh the '80s, cometh the Cadbury's Wispa. Big trouble in Rowntreeland as the potential Aero spoiler was worriedly picked over. Luckily the two-year gestation period Cadbury took to get the Wispa going nationwide allowed Rowntree to remake the Aero in its image. By September of 1982, gone was the six-segmented flat format, a bumpy chocolate version of the traffic-calming measures in a well-to-do Cotswold village. In came the handy ingot size. In the process, something – no one was quite sure what – changed. The chocolate had become softer. No, the bubbles were bigger. No, it's the taste... It scarcely mattered, as the new bar more than held its own against the Bournville parvenu. But even today, plenty of former stalwart Aerovians feel slighted by the changes, their enzyme glands no longer stimulated in quite the same way.

*AZTEC

This is a tale of two cultural cornerstones. On the one hand, the mighty Quetzalcoatl, feathered serpent god of the ancient Aztecs, who gave his people the sacred gift of chocolate via a beam of heavenly light, bringing them universal wisdom and Type 2 diabetes. (Sadly, the one bit of knowledge that might have been some use, namely

Opposite: A sign of civilisation. Aztec (1967), swiftly sacrificed to the gods of chocolate nostalgia.

Below: Instigating a Mexican crave. Safety-pin propaganda on behalf of Cadbury.

9

'If you see these Spanish blokes with big shiny helmets, run like the clappers,' slipped the feathered one's mind.) In the blue corner, there's the equally legendary rival to the Mars bar, opportunistically cooked up by Cadbury in a lean period and promoted with a travelogue-swish TV campaign filmed at one of your actual Mexican temples, only to vanish mysteriously four years later. The former lived on for centuries in folk memory and overpriced Acapulco gift shops. The latter enjoyed a similarly fertile afterlife, becoming the de facto nostalgic touchstone for the first wave of alternative comedians (Ben Elton's swing-top bin was so long unemptied it had 'Aztec wrappers in the bottom').

It's perhaps fair to say that Elton's championing of fair-trade didn't tally too well with the Aztec's imperialistic undertones, a state of affairs not helped by the life-size cardboard warrior chieftains installed in newsagents the nation over, to the innocent delight of kids who'd gleefully perform a culturally inaccurate whooping war dance around them. All this happened, of course, while the Milky Bar kid was doing his bit for the Native North Americans. To complete the continental clean sweep, the 1980s, when you'd have thought people would have

calmed down a bit, saw the launch of the otherwise unremarkable Rowntree's Inca. We could, of course, all be very smart and ironic about such things by the time the Aztec made the slightest of slight returns in the year 2000.

*BOUNTY

There was always something indefinably odd about the Bounty. It wasn't the bar itself. 'Tender coconut, moist with pure syrup, lavish with thick chocolate.' Nothing unusual about that. We'd been here before in 1950, with Rowntree's ill-fated Cokeroon bar. Maybe it's the way the Bounty featured two bars in one pack, without making a

Opposite: Dessication's what you need.
Bounty (1951).

11

song and dance about it. Always suspicious when a chocolate bar keeps something like that to itself. And the way it did it – not side by side, but in series, with a little jerry-built piece of black waxed cardboard guttering underneath to take up the inevitable slack, leading uncertain youngsters with fond memories of the rice paper on the bottoms of macaroons to try to digest the whole thing. All most irregular.

Then there were the adverts. 'A Taste of Paradise' had been around since the mid-'60s, and was fairly self-explanatory. Coconut = tropical. Dead posh, like. Fair enough. The problems began in 1977, with the 'Bounty hunters' TV campaign, showing a weird tribe of well-groomed, lightly tanned Caucasians lounging about on a tropical island somewhere, having left civilisation behind. How could they look that good out there? Especially when they existed entirely on Bountys?

Not only that, they made the bars themselves. Somehow. We saw a coconut being deftly cleft in twain. Then a sheaf of perfectly wrapped bars floated down a limpid stream on a raft of palm leaves, for the tribe's womenfolk to pick out and chew absent-mindedly under a waterfall. The intervening stages of manufacture were missing. Where were the grunts shredding the coconut? How did they get hold of the syrup? Whither the

glycerol processing plant? And the guttering mystery remained. Worse still, the original flute-led musical backing from Howard '*The Snowman*' Blake now featured scene-setting lyrics. 'The Bow-own-tee-hee HUN-ters, are here/ They're searching for PAR-a-dise...' trilled a woman who sounded constantly worried she'd chosen a falsetto too high to sustain. This explained nothing.

After 1978, this fair-trade wonder had to compete with the Rowntree's Cabana, which added caramel and chopped glacé cherries to the coconut mix, testing the retentive powers of even the strongest stomach. So they made attempts to assimilate into the real world, acquiring catamarans and scuba gear and moving into the more general 'sun-kissed lifestyle' aspirational bracket loved by lazy Martini account holders and Duran Duran. Structural improvements in wrapper engineering rendered the guttering redundant. The tremulous falsetto became a schmaltzy cover of 'Try a Little Tenderness'. The message was: 'Hey, it's okay! We're not strange at all any more!' Nevertheless, the Bounty is still looked at askance by your average British consumer. Still, it could have been worse: in America it's called Mounds.

*CADBURY'S CARAMEL

Cadbury had a big year in 1976. On the downside, there was the Rowntree's Yorkie. More positively, there was the Montreal Winter Olympics, all over which the Goodies appeared in TV ads urging hungry kids to swap ten Cadbury wrappers (oh, and £3.60) for a transistor radio in exciting blue denim!

Opposite: Hare necessities. Cadbury's Caramel (1976).

Below: 'Hey Mr Bee, why are you buzzing around?' A Baloo-influenced work ethic for the dole age via the Cadbury's Caramel bunny, circa 1979.

13

Then there was the launch of the Cadbury's Caramel.

You could tell this was a classy bar. For a start, it was frighteningly expensive, even in those times of vertiginous price rises. It was also very neat, each section being a little sculpted pillow of chocolate, delicately engraved with the Cadbury livery. Let there be no idle talk of 'chunks' here. All terribly sophisticated, very grown-up… and a tad dull, to be honest. This product needed sexing up.

Enter five-foot jobbing actress Miriam Margolyes, who took one of the least promising briefs ever ('Right, so you're this lazy, but saucy, West Country rabbit with a chocolate obsession…') and turned in thirty seconds of sub-Bristol vocal smouldering that was destined for immortality. The cartoon blurred the line over who the product was aimed at slightly. Was it responsible to tell children 'arses are there to be sat on, have some chocolate', via a buck-toothed erotic trade unionist? Nevertheless, a surprisingly timeless campaign was created.

Cadbury took their own advice and took it easy, letting the anthropomorphic amour carry the weight. The bar's sales never troubled the top ten, but the 'exclusive' price kept it afloat. In 1993, enter the Galaxy Caramel.

Panic on the streets of Bournville! Well, okay, a bit of a rebadge and a new recipe. It saw off the competition, but it's hard not to view this most successful of also-ran bars as a bit too much in temperament like its skiving mascot, and too little like her industrious, if slightly thick, woodland pals.

*CARAMAC

N amed after Halifax-based toffee tycoon John Mackintosh rather than the American beat poet author of *On the Road*, Kerouac – no, hang on – Caramac nonetheless seems to have had most in common with the iconoclast, hippie, jazz musings of the latter. First, for an entire decade or more, it defied all marketing logic by continuing to sell

Opposite: The Eat Generation. Alternative caramel confectionery in the form of Caramac (1959).

Below: Hey, have you heard the one about your statutory rights? Rowntree Mackintosh aims for the funny bone in a 1982 comic ad. 15

without a single commercial spot to its name. (Then 1991 saw a TV relaunch of the 'I was here all along' ilk, backed by a pointed, almost sardonic, version of the Tremeloes' 'Silence Is Golden'.)

Second, there was something so gritty in the texture, a viscous fudginess in that original recipe which was so very redolent of melting, syrupy brown nuggets of street heroin. Caramac felt like the detritus, sweepings from the post-war factory floor of Rowntree's production line, scooped up, tipped into a vat and boiled down into something altogether more... well, moreish. But, of course, it wasn't. Far from a happy accident, it was a careful concoction of sweetened condensed milk, butter, treacle and so on, intended to replicate as closely as possible the experience of chomping through its cocoa-based cousins.

In fact, like the best British home cooking, its appeal was driven by economics, austerity and nostalgia. Caramac was a stodgy Sunday sticky toffee pudding turned into a thin, anaemic bar. A bar that, for all the love and attention lavished on its preparation, could never call itself chocolate. Neither fish nor fowl, Caramac sought mainstream acceptance by arranged marriages to other, more established brands. Hence Carawheat, a Jacob's biscuit covered in a golden Caramac layer, and a later

Breakaway version. Though what really took the biscuit was the cheeky twenty-first-century hook-up with a certain four-fingered wafer snack (presumably because of the pleasing, nursery rhyme result). All together now: Kit Kat Caramac, give the dog a bone...

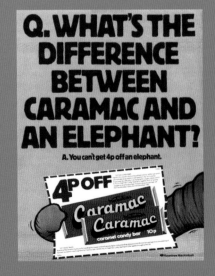

Q. WHAT'S THE DIFFERENCE BETWEEN CARAMAC AND AN ELEPHANT?

A. You can't get 4p off an elephant.

4P OFF

Caramac
Caramac

caramel candy bar   10p

*CHEWITS

In 1965 corporate financier and asset stripper Jimmy Goldsmith, bored with outrageous takeover bids and fending off bankruptcy, boldly chose to move into the confectionery business. He formed Cavenham Foods, named after the family estate, from an amalgamation of the flagging Carsons & Goodies of Bristol, Parkinsons of Doncaster and Hollands of Southport.

Opposite: Here's looking at chew, kid. Triumphantly post-imperial Chewits (1965).

Below: Alternative muncher monster name suggestions: Chew Hefner, Pepe Le Chew, Nerys Chews, Chiouxsie & The Banshees, Chewy Chase.

17

This last was at the time best known for its one penny Arrow bar (advertised in the '70s by a precocious Bonnie Langford, almost certainly giving rise to the phrase 'she can't act for toffee') but a new fondant chew would put the company – not to mention Barrow-in-Furness bus depot – firmly on the map.

Chewits were stickier, more sugary and more solid than their nearest rivals Opal Fruits – so much so that they required special machinery from Germany to manufacture and wrap. A special technique was also necessary to smuggle them into your mouth unseen during double maths lessons. The earliest range offered a choice of strawberry, blackcurrant, orange or banana flavours and were packaged in a mottled camouflage design which made them look a little like military refugees from a particularly effeminate NAAFI. By far their greatest sales boost, however, was delivered in 1976 by the Aardman-animated Godzilla-like star of the 'Muncher' adverts.

In these, a giant Plasticine Pleistocene chewed his way through some b-movie spoofing scenery, before being quelled by the taste of the altogether more satisfying Chewits (wrappers and all), literally off the back of

a lorry. Later ads highlighted the creature's claymation capers at a selection of tasty international landmarks (the aforementioned bus terminus, the Taj Mahal and the Empire State Building) and a raucous rampage through wartime London, much to the chagrin of the local ARP warden.

Chewits were popular with pauper and pregnant princess alike. In 1981 an expectant Diana was caught short of cash at a Gloucestershire sweet shop after unexpected cravings for a pack of the strawberry flavour – a story deemed bafflingly headline-worthy by the *Daily Mirror*. Meanwhile, the penniless tearaways of Merseyside knew exactly which bins to raid for misshapen and discarded rejects at the rear of the Chewits factory on Virginia Street. Let them eat cack, you might say.

Jimmy Goldsmith became Sir James in 1976. In the midst of issuing writs for defamation against Richard Ingrams's *Private Eye*, he moved control of his interests to Paris and privatised the confectionery and bakery businesses. Ironically, the Muncher dinosaur (renamed Chewie the Chewitsaurus by new owners Leaf in 1989) lived to fight another day, long after Cavenham and Hollands themselves became extinct.

I'M A Chewits MUNCHER!

On the lolly packaging:
Count Dracula's
TRACE-A-FACE
BLACK AND WHITE
ICED LOLLY WITH JELLY

*COUNT DRACULA'S DEADLY SECRET

Kids today, eh? Addled with filthy music, junk food and daft fashions, and well before they reach their teenage years. Why can't they just grow up naturally, like we used to? I blame these raunchy new pop stars. Like that David Essex. And the Rollers, they're wrong 'uns. And as for

Opposite: The original Dracula's Secret, before it was classified 'deadly', to make it sound more scary.

Below: Love at first bite. Wall's Dracula (1981), ultimately resurrected in 2013.

19

that rag *Whizzer and Chips*...' It's the eternal refrain, but you heard it in the *Daily Mirror* first, when in the early '70s they identified the 'Weenies', an ominous new, conspicuously consuming, old-before-their-time pre-teen generation. While perusing life-size posters of Kenny, these reprobates subsisted on a diet of Trebor Blobs, spaghetti hoops and 'iced lollipops – especially the "frighteners" like Count Dracula's Deadly Secret'. Horror again! The nation's moral guardians would no doubt have preferred a series of ice lollies themed around the Duke of Edinburgh's Award Scheme or Hard Sums, but it was not to be.

The spine-tingling ice under analysis came from Wall's: 'a creation of "black as night" water ice with a concealed centre of ice cream as bright as the moon when it's full'. Such florid descriptions were part and parcel of the horror genre of course, and someone in the publicity department relished being HP Lovecraft for a day. The design team went that extra mile, too: the following year, the Count was on the receiving end of the industry's first focus-group makeover, after a panel of kids demanded he be made 'even more deadly looking' with an additional core of strawberry jelly. Food and fanbase in perfect, fiendish harmony.

Children's enthusiasm being the mercurial thing it is, though,

the Count only saw a handful of summers before Wall's saw fit to hammer a stick through his heart. You can't keep a good vamp down, though, and he rose again in 1981, this time just as 'Dracula', but in glorious, chiselled 3D. 'The first ever 3D lolly,' in fact, 'complete with protruding fangs and talons and appropriate strawberry colouring.' This masterpiece of the ice moulder's art was cast from a model by one Bob Donaldson, 'who has also been commissioned to sculpt for the Queen'. European aristocracy has connections everywhere, even beyond the grave.

*CREME EGG

Though various fondant-filled eggs had been produced by Cadbury since 1923, it wasn't until decimalisation that the Brummie confectioners finally cracked it with the consumer. That consummate assemblage of foil wrapper, chocolate shell, thick sugary albumen and all-important yolk centre debuted amid precious little fanfare.

Opposite: Easter bon-bonnet. Cadbury's Creme Egg (1971).

Below: Foiled again? Cadbury makes it difficult for treasure hunters to poach themselves a golden egg.

21

(Readers in Scotland had their own chocolate-filled egg.)

A short TV spot encouraging the customary Jennings-like schoolchildren to overwhelm shopkeepers with demands for '6,000 Creme Eggs, please' failed to take into account the limited means of the audience. But the marketers persisted and eventually hatched a television campaign based around a reworking of Cole Porter's genteel and only slightly racist song, 'Let's Do It', which saw all manner of shy debutantes, maiden aunts and girls in France falling for the irresistible charms of the ovoid snack. Impressionable kids scrambled to empty their piggy banks and helped boost

sales from around 50 million in the mid-'70s to nearly 200 million by the early '80s.

In 1984 Cadbury's creative agency, Triangle, no doubt spurred on by the success of *Masquerade*, Kit Williams's kids' book, conceived an unashamedly derivative national treasure hunt for twelve golden eggs. Caskets were buried in far-flung corners of the countryside (though one, discovered accidentally, nearly blew the lid off the whole enterprise) and Creme Egg fans were invited to send off for, and solve, the *Conundrum*. Within three months, Cadbury had to call a press conference to halt overzealous punters digging up stone circles, hill forts and Christian

Below: Scotch egg. Cadbury's Border Creme Egg (1970) eschews sausage and breadcrumbs in favour of a chocolate fondant centre.

Opposite: The yolk's on you. Cadbury's Easter catalogue leads with a 'cracking' pun for 1986.

burial sites in search of the £10,000 ('Garrards certified retail value') eggs. As far as slogans go, 'Stop looking on or around Pendle Hill and the Wrekin' is about as off-brand as you can get.

However, all this hedge-hopping hadn't gone unnoticed and Cadbury's rivals soon poached the egg idea for their own retail lines. Rowntree introduced both the Toffee Mallow and Fresh Minty Egg (in 1982), and Terry's hit back with the Nutcracker (ostensibly the same shape, only wrinkled, filled with caramel and nuts), then, in 1988, the ill-advised 'indulgent novelty' that was the Pyramint. Aimed at an older market, and fabulously advertised by the voice-artist dream-team of Leslie Phillips and Kenneth Williams, both hamming it up for all they were worth with an Egyptian mummy, it was a massive flop.

Too large, too unwieldy and too messy to eat, Pyramint barely

survived three years before being resurrected in a four-segment bar format and then quietly interred for a million years. The Creme Egg, however, continued to grow (not literally, it has genuinely always been the same size). In 1986 the question 'How do you eat yours?' was raised, backed by an in-store promotion inviting shoppers to collect fifteen wrappers and send in for a free 'computer-produced personality analysis'. **(RESULT: YOU ARE BEREFT OF LOVE AND FILL THE ACHING HOLE THAT REMAINS WITH CHOCOLATE.)** Then, in 1992, Cadbury's very own Easter Bunny laid her first Caramel Egg (again, not literally; that would be the weirdest cartoon ever). The nest, as they say, is history.

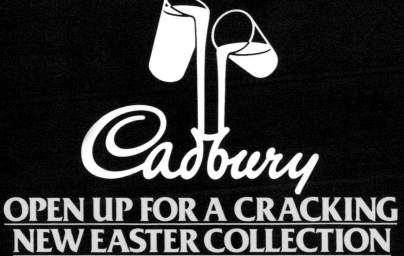

Cadbury

OPEN UP FOR A CRACKING
NEW EASTER COLLECTION

EASTER
1986

*CRUNCHIE

Honeycomb, cinder toffee, call it what you will, it's as old as the hills. It's easy to make: get some sugar and corn syrup extremely bloody hot, bung in some baking powder, stand well back, and there you have it. Or rather, there you have irregular lumps of it. It's how you tame the fragile honeycomb into a sleek polyhedron that's the tricky part.

Aussie manufacturer Hoadley's started squaring the brittle in 1918 with the Violet Crumble. The down-under spies at Fry's reported this back to their Keynsham HQ, and a race was on to replicate it. Early attempts were unreliable, Fry's having to employ women specially to solder snapped bars back together with bunsen burners, but eventually a nifty system of cutting the slabs with a high-pressure jet of oil solved the problem. Add a distinctive heavy foil wrapper to stop the honeycomb going soft, and it's Crunchie ahoy.

It was slow to take off, despite some early product placement in horsey kids' book *National Velvet*, though after the Second World War it was popular enough for Rowntree to float a short-lived rival, Cracknel Block. The '60s saw it really embed into the national psyche – by '68 *Observer* hacks were writing 'that's the way the Crunchie crumbles' when casting about for a with-it-sounding cliché.

By the '80s it was everywhere, repackaged in shiny gold and sponsoring Five Star and Billy Ocean. Though what really got it noticed was a strange daily ad campaign in 1987, wherein an automatic wall-calendar sombrely recorded the changing days of the week, as a rather glum voice mused, 'Not long till Friday.' Come the weekend, this low-key teaser was revealed as the beginning of the Thank Crunchie

It's Friday campaign, which gave rise to two decades of frenetic fun in the name of burnt sugar. Modern advertising, you see, all very clever. And slightly more appropriate than associating children's chocolate with the man who sang 'Get Outta My Dreams, Get Into My Car'.

*CURLY WURLY

C adbury entered the 1970s in a reflective mood. Mars was the problem. Mars's big-hitters – filled bars in the Marathon, Mars or Milky Way mould – were cleaning up, while Cadbury's sedate blocks were primarily successful with only the older, and significantly less impulsive, customer. No one bought and scoffed three bars of

Opposite: Cadbury's make with the 'miles of chewy toffee.' Curly Wurly (1970).

27

Fruit 'n' Nut in an afternoon break. (Or at least, if they did, they kept quiet about it.) Cadbury already had the Crunchie under Fry's imprimatur, but recent innovations had met with varied results. Their best shot was the Aztec, but even that was losing to the celestially named behemoths from Slough. Cloning Mars products was a fool's errand, so Cadbury's technicians started thinking outside the bar. One outlandish design, a braided lattice of three caramel laces, seemed to fit the bill. A pleasingly wacky shape inside, and it dwarfed its rivals on the shelves by dint of sheer scale: as Malcolm Tucker reminisced in *The Thick of It*, 'the size of a small ladder'.

This was the confectioner's Holy Grail: give them less, but convince them it's more. It worked a treat. A focus group of 100 children were given a bar to munch, then asked if they'd rather have a sixpence or another Curly Wurly. Only seven plumped for the cash, but history doesn't record whether that was due to the new bar, or the knowledge that, with decimalisation round the corner, chocolate was probably a better investment than a moribund tanner.

The bar launched in a blaze of publicity. TV ads featured Terry Scott as a Bunterish schoolboy causing good-natured, sugar-fuelled havoc in assorted public buildings, in every commercial break ITV had to offer between noon and teatime. Never before had chocolate been so heavily marketed: the sweet old days of George Lazenby stomping down a gangplank with an outsize replica Fry's bar had given way to an orgy of mass media exposure, making the Curly Wurly, in Cadbury's humble estimation, 'the success story of post-war confectionery'.

Such success, inevitably, spawned imitators. Within two years, homages appeared in Canada, Germany, Japan and the US (where Mars confused a generation of holidaying Brits by naming their faux-Wurly Marathon). Nothing could beat the original, though, not even the 1980s scrapping of the decreasingly schoolboyish Scott in favour of a frankly bizarre campaign featuring a moose in American football gear and a spookily silent child. All very odd, but the Curly Wurly was now the institution Cadbury had longed for, and the kids wrote off in their thousands to East Molesey for Curly Wurly Club packs and badges. You only needed ten wrappers to join, too. Terry Scott could've managed that in an afternoon.

*DAIRY MILK

The first solid block of edible chocolate appeared in the UK in 1847, courtesy of the Fry brothers of Bristol. Making one that tasted nice was a tougher matter, mainly to do with milk's tendency to go off at the drop of a hat. In the end, slow-and-steady George Cadbury won the race. Eight years in development, his Highland Milk bar tasted

Opposite: Class and a half. Cadbury's Dairy Milk (1905) experimenting with size and typeface changes throughout the 70s and 80s.

Below: Everyone's a Fruit & Nut case. A succinct name for Cadbury's raisin and almond bar (1928).

29

good enough to beat the Swiss. It was renamed Dairy Maid, and shortly after renamed again to Dairy Milk, on the advice of a Plymouth shopkeeper. Boasting '1½ glasses in every ½ lb', it was launched in 1905 to great success.

A year later, the plain Bournville appeared, followed by Fruit and Nut in 1928, and Whole Nut two years after that. Even Hitler couldn't stop its advance: one press ad in the bleak days of 1939 advised: 'The habit of taking a block of Cadbury's Dairy Milk per day has been medically recommended as a sensible personal precaution for this autumn and winter.'

By 1960, the usual suspects lined up alongside flavours of pineapple, peppermint, coffee, marzipan, strawberry and the intriguingly vague 'mild dessert'. The late 1960s was full of entreaties for Britons to 'award yourself the CDM'. A nice idea, but a bit staid for such a forward-looking time, and in the early '70s it became more wistful still, asking punters if, in this modern, synthetic world, wasn't it good to know that 'there's always Cadbury's Dairy Milk'?

Then in 1976 Rowntree launched their Yorkie, and such statements suddenly looked very optimistic. Hit even harder, Cadbury returned to the 'glass and a half' tagline they'd abandoned in the mid-'60s, and fought the lorry drivers of York with Cilla Black putting a chunk in her cheek on the top deck of a Blackpool tram. Meanwhile Frank Muir twisted his tongue round tales of bucolic Fruit and Nut mania to the strains of Tchaikovsky, and a scarily omnipotent calypso band informed unwitting citizens of the world that, regarding nuts (whole hazelnuts), Cadbury take them and they cover them in chocolate.

To seal this fightback, the bars themselves also became thicker (and pricier) once more. The ever-changing sizes were in part due to the rocketing price of cocoa, which increased tenfold between 1973 and 1977. Cadbury circled their wagons ever tighter, badging everything under the Dairy Milk label. This made sound business sense, but some of the fun had been let out, children of the future denied the Dickensian pleasure of bursting into a sweet shop and asking for 'an Oliver Twist, two Tiffins and a Big Wig, please!'

*DIME

The Scandinavians, for some reason, have never been in a hurry to export any of their consumer goodies. There's a fish-canning company in Göteborg who, had they shown more international ambition in the '70s, might now not be the world's second-most well-known Abba. Similarly, the UK had to wait nearly thirty years for the

Opposite: Brother, can you spare a Dime (1953)?

Below: Ruddy hell, it's Harry and... Harry? Enfield coins it in, circa 1993.

31

affordable home accessories and tricky-to-assemble furniture of IKEA to arrive in its giant, out-of-town industrial parks. So it was that, in 1982, Barker and Dobson (of Victory V fame) and Marabou of Sweden finally brokered a historic deal to distribute the latter's crunchy, buttery, almondy sliver of a bar to a grateful British public. The Dajm had arrived, in the scantiest of chocolate coats. (Hurrah! Schnapps all round, etc. Although, er, we're going to have to take another look at that name, guys.)

Impossible to describe to anyone who hadn't yet eaten their first, a fact later exploited for Harry Enfield's winning television campaign, the rechristened Dime materialised in tuck shops almost entirely without branding 'push' but with an attractive 15p price tag attached instead. It proved to be a cracking success, so an emboldened Marabou raided their cupboards for other lines that might yield a high exchange rate on the confectionery currency converter. However, neither the twenty-two piece, prosaically named Milk Chocolate Roll, nor the sickly sweet butter-cream-crisp Delight bar caught the public imagination in the same way. Disillusionment set in and, after a skanky American drive-in-themed ad ('Dynamite Dime') failed to blow up, Marabou took their business elsewhere.

Barker and Dobson fell immediately into bed with Ritter Schokoladefabrik of West Germany and began supplying the unusually filled, but resealable, Sport brand chocolate blocks to off-licences ('snaps open for action, folds back for protection'). United Biscuits sealed the deal for UK Dime distribution and, within years, had the nation shouting, 'Oi, nutter!', 'Armadillos!' and other such advert catchphrase nonsense. They never did quite nail the product description, though. Current Norwegian owners Kraft's website probably comes closest, putting it, via Google translation software, as 'the small bent piece of chocolate glaze'. Quite right too.

*DOUBLE AGENTS

In the post-Spangles cold war of boiled sweet selling, finding a unique hook to excite the kids represented an excellent tactical advantage. Whether it be a new flavour, shape or texture, the trade secrets of the confectionery manufacturers were locked behind massive iron factory gates. Of course industrial espionage went on, but outright

Opposite: Boiled sweet Burgess. Trebor Double Agents (1977), the spy that came out of a mould.

33

Slugworth-style stealing of another company's ideas was frowned upon – though not so, apparently, if you were pinching them from outside the industry.

So it was that Trebor's Double Agents came to be advertised by what can – at best – be called an homage to Antonio Prohías's Spy vs. Spy cartoons, as seen in *MAD* magazine since the early '60s. On TV, exhibiting a spectacular misunderstanding of the meaning of 'secret agent', two animated infiltrators, Boris (aka Black Spy) and Carruthers (aka White Spy), attempted to hijack a shipment of the sweets in broad daylight using an assortment of Acme bombs. While the Concorde-nosed imagery was heavily Prohías-influenced, the action was pure Warner Bros.

The cloak-and-dagger pair also appeared in a series of 'Psst... kids' collect-and-send comic offers hawking such essential intelligence-gathering ephemera as a fingerprint kit, a twelve-cap revolver and an iron-on, glow-in-the-dark transfer. It was all exciting stuff for a budding Anthony Blunt or infant-class Mata Hari. Sadly, the rather more prosaic reality of the sweets themselves was that they were

merely the latest in a long line of Trebor's procession of soft-centred tubes, the new packaging adding extra edge to the 'two flavours in one' conceit (chocolate and lime, strawberry and cream, raspberry and sherbet, and so on).

Printed on the underside of the pack were obligatory top-secret 'spy hints' of dubious practical use for actual undercover operations, such as using lemon juice as invisible ink, making a spy-ring stamp out of a potato, or disguising your appearance by stuffing a cushion under your coat. Further messages were hidden inside the individual wax paper wrappers for conspiratorial code-cracking sessions back at base – often a home-made den constructed from two chairs and your mum's spare sheets.

Double Agents appeared at the height of UK spy mania, with James Bond still at the peak of his powers, seducing Barbara Bach and audiences alike to the tune of Carly Simon's 'Nobody Does It Better'. From the Union Jack parachute opening to shark tank battle finale, *The Spy Who Loved Me* is one of the more enjoyable romps of the franchise. It also marked the first appearance of Richard Kiel's steel-toothed henchman, Jaws, a villain who must surely have spent too much time sucking sweets and not enough time visiting the dentist.

*DOUBLE DECKER

Meals on wheels, as the giveaway badge would have it. Double Decker was yet another sortie into what the product developers termed 'substantial' snacking territory. A slightly coffee-flavoured nougat layer floated above a palate-gouging base of cornflakes, rice and (until the mid-'80s) raisins suspended in a chocolate

Opposite: Brum brum. Birmingham's Double Decker (1976), featuring the original raisin recipe.

35

matrix. Clearly the name was a marketing retrofit to the technology that enabled such choccy bar apartheid but it immediately invoked a definitive symbol of Britishness. Tall, uniquely constructed and recognised all over the world. Not buying one was bally well unpatriotic, what?

So who better to embody such sterling stoicism than satirist, comedian and actor Willie Rushton, jabbering his way through a solo 'crunchy or chewy?' debate on the TV ads? Well, er, maybe Cliff Richard. Or Melvin Hayes. Or anyone else from *Summer Holiday* that the public might more immediately identify with a rear-loading Routemaster to help promote this between-meals bus fare. (Typical! You wait ages for a likely celeb to endorse your product then three come along at once.)

In 1983 there emerged Dougie, the Double Decker dog, a predictably furry man-in-a-suit mascot who toured the country giving away bars at the likes of Pontin's, before it was decided he should go away 'to live on a special farm'. The concurrent telly campaign featured the incongruous arrival of a Cadbury-liveried bus at unsuspecting punters' places of work just when they felt 'a bit peckish'. Convenient for elevenses, yes, but pity the poor pensioners already aboard, hawked hither and thither on their journey to the post office.

Sold as 'the double filling bar for the double filling feeling' Double Decker was no doubt the favourite of innuendo-loving bus drivers everywhere. Yet, where were the specially designed chocolate bars for other RMT union members? London Underground staff arguably had the tube of Smarties, and road freight was all wrapped up in Yorkie, but mainline rail, shipping and offshore, or any number of other transport-sector workers, were criminally ignored. In fact, it may only be comic association with the cheeky clippies and malingering conductors of LWT's *On the Buses* that allowed the Double Decker to remain in service. Although the TV show was long gone by the time Double Decker rolled up, Cadbury's PR bods more than missed a trick not reuniting Stan, Jack, Olive et al. for one final excursion to adland, especially considering Blakey even came equipped with his own snack-friendly slogan-cum-gag, i.e. 'Did you eat that Double Decker, Inspector?' 'No, I 'ate you, Butler!'

*EXTRA STRONG MINTS

There's always been a fine line between mint and medicine. At the extremes of mintiness, indulgent pleasure transforms into a tongue-bashing riot of 'good for what ails you' macho flavour riding. If it's not hurting, it's not working, and all that. Victorian strong mints even sounded medicinal: take two Altoids and see me in the

Opposite: National Service for your tastebuds: Sharps Extra Strong Mints (1972).

Below: Sky high QI guy? TV advert, circa 1984.

37

morning. But the titan of twentieth-century confectionery masochism was the Extra Strong Mint.

Made by Sharps of York since 1937, it really took off decades later, when a national ad campaign asserted, 'You either love them or you hate them!' Throughout the '70s a formerly niche product rose to challenge the Polo itself at the top of the sales tree. TV ads came thick and fast. One proclaimed, 'They'll blow your socks off!' while an assortment of folk had their business interrupted by just such an eruption of the half hose. Later Graham Chapman fed the mints to victims of a medieval witch trial, and a pre-omnipotence Stephen Fry used his mint-heated breath to power a hot-air balloon over the Alps. All over the country folk snapped up the hotter mints for mouth deodorisers, anti-smoking aids and to help 'driving concentration'.

Aside from a strong mint launched by Bassett in 1983, rival firms were slow to take a bite out of the extra strong market, but when they did, it was a deluge. Fisherman's Friend producers Lofthouse were the first to pitch up in 1988, with a minty take on their core product claimed to be hotter than Sharps by a noticeable margin. Later that same year Rowntree weighed in with XXX, a dead spit for Sharps' product in size, shape and even wrapper. Trebor, owner of Sharps, called foul. This was a spoiler, they claimed, to stop their Extra Strongs taking over from Polo as the nation's favourite mint. They forced a change of packaging and barred the new mint from their wholesale chain Moffatt's. Rowntree retaliated with an unprecedented £2 million, five-week ad campaign with an appropriate Cold War theme. Then in 1989 Needler's entered the market with their black-clad ESM, boasting a 'pure white heat' that was 15 per cent hotter than Trebor's. They didn't stay the pace, but Sharps and Rowntree continued to slug it out, and have maintained an uneasy (and, for the unwary shopper, confusing) détente ever since.

*FAB

Lyons Maid, always ahead of the game, jumped on board the starship Telly Tie-In long before man even set foot on the moon. A hook-up with Gerry Anderson's puppet series *Fireball XL5* in 1963 led to the launch of Zoom, a three-stage fruity rocket aimed at viewers catching the space bug. The following year's Sea Jet (available in strawberry, vanilla, lemon or orange flavours) quenched the *Stingray* fans' thirst for a lolly of their own, and the chocolate orange stylings of Orbit were paired up with Cary Grant soundalike, *Captain Scarlet*, in 1968.

However, it was the arrival of International Rescue's London agent, Lady Penelope, that finally boosted Lyons Maid's sales into the stratosphere. Designed to appeal to Britain's 3 million girls under fifteen, the Fab lolly teamed a strawberry skirt with a vanilla ice cream top, and a chocolate coat decorated with multi-coloured sprinkles. The resultant ensemble not only shared the elegant femininity and icy centre of Thunderbirds' socialite spy, but also took its name from the number plate on her powder-pink Rolls-Royce, FAB 1.

A Space: 1999 lolly in 1976 completed Lyons Maid's association with Andersonia, although the cult TV obsession continued. *The Six Million Dollar Man* graced the wrapper of the Bionic Lolly (RRP a paltry 8p), and The Fonz was a fittingly cool front man for *Happy Days* in 1979. Wall's too eventually succumbed to the lure of celebrity and released a Fab clone of their own (with the addition of an orange jelly centre in

a dismissive, hand-waving gesture to any accusations of 'passing off'), but only because they'd secured the important ice cream rights to... the kids from *Fame*.

The Fab lolly remains synonymous with 1960s' swinging retro kitsch, yet it has been in steady production for over forty years. It almost always experiences a resurgence in popularity every time *Thunderbirds* is repeated (memorably, in 1991, amid Tracy Island play set 'toy of the year' fever). Another timely endorsement, by the quite literally lolly-pop-tastic DJs Smashie and Nicey (courtesy of Harry Enfield and Paul Whitehouse), maintained the Fab's cosmic and comic clout with the kids.

Less successful, however, was the psychedelic Luv, notable only for a fleeting appearance by the then jobbing thespian David Bowie in its singalong 1969 advert. Perhaps the lolly wouldn't have bombed if Lyons Maid had chosen to soundtrack it with a song he composed the very same week – instead, 'Space Oddity' provided Bowie with his first number one a matter of months later – but who was to know that inside the fresh-faced boy was a future Thin White Duke? It's not as if he dressed like Lady Gaga at the time. It's true: the stars look very different today.

*FLAKE

Here come the girls! Some twenty-odd of them down the years, in fact; each one winsomely wrapping her lips around a fat, ribbed shaft of sweet, delicious chocolate in a series of adverts increasingly intent on steaming up the glasses of nervous, starch-collared middle managers the land over. Such simmering sensuality may have been

Opposite: Breaking the mould. Flake (1920) – as unique as a fingerprint, they say. But tastier.

Below: Like water for chocolate. Flake ads get steamy circa 1991.   41

lost on runny-nosed rug rats, but dads were reportedly consumed on the spot by a terrible lust, which must have been quite off-putting if you were trying to make a cuppa in the middle of *3-2-1*.

In fact, back in the early black and white era, Flake girls fantasised about nothing more exciting than waterfalls, pony-trekking and 'sixpence-worth of heaven', which is hardly bonkbuster territory. (No mention of a tuppence, for starters.) It took the creative muscle of Norman Icke (also responsible for the Curly Wurly and Milk Tray ads) and Ronnie Bond (not the Troggs ex-drummer) to forge the cast-iron classic 'Only the crumbliest, flakiest chocolate' jingle and remind us it 'tastes like chocolate never tasted before', although they singularly failed to point out that it also drops crumbs down your shirt and onto Mum's best cushions like never before. Presumably the Flake girls took to so seductively unwrapping their choc bars al fresco 'cos they were sick and tired of being nagged about leaving tell-tale specks on the sofa.

Thenceforth, colour television was treated to a heavy rotation of soft-focus semi-erotic vignettes set in fields bursting with poppies or sunflowers, and plots involving runaway gypsy caravans, untethered rowing boats, and sudden summer downpours. (All the better for drenching those doe-eyed beauties in their clingy, sheer and see-through clothes, eh, lads?) Through the '70s and '80s a succession of sultry models succumbed to the Flake's mouth-watering chocolate charms, including former Miss World Eva Rueber-Staier (whose ad was pulled, such was its perceived lasciviousness), royal squeeze Catrina Skepper (trading in Prince Andrew for something slightly less ostentatious) and, in 1987, Debbie Leng, scantily clad and draped, legs akimbo, in the window seat of a chateau while a gecko scuttled inexplicably across an unattended phone. (The lizard 'suggested the exotic' claimed Icke later. Leng herself went on to hook up with Roger Taylor of Queen fame. Draw your own conclusions there.) Arguably the best-remembered of the ads, however, featured Scouse Lisa Stansfield lookalike Rachel Brown luxuriating in an overflowing bath. Prime spoof-fodder for the likes of Jasper Carrott ('Here's your problem, love. It's Flake wrappers in the plughole'), the ad also attained legendary playground status when rumours circulated that 'the girl in it overdosed on Ecstasy and ended up in the nuthouse'. (Chinese whispers, as it turns out: Brown was hospitalised

after allegedly being spiked with Class As at a birthday party and made a full recovery.)

However, that flooded Venetian bathroom coincidentally harks back to Cadbury's initial inspiration for the Flake, as it was a lowly factory employee who spotted that excess chocolate spilling from the moulds cascaded down in a stream of thin sheets, creating a distinctive texture. Never, it must be said, has an industrial accident been repackaged so successfully and sold so pruriently. Mars's similarly phallic chocolate log, the Ripple, failed to chop down the mighty Flake, possibly because it didn't have a powerhouse creative marketing team behind it, possibly because it was noticeably that bit smaller, or possibly just because it rhymed with 'nipple'. A rebrand in 1987 saw Ripple embraced into the premium Galaxy fold, and 1992 added further length and girth to the bar, making it immediately more popular with women. Tsk! Typical. And, though even Cadbury have long since axed A-rated allusions to fellatio from their branding campaign, it will be a good while yet before those Flake ads drop out of any bloke's top ten sexiest/sexist formative moments.

For goodness sake!

Cadbury's

99 Flake

WIN £1,000 EVERY WEEK!

DURING THE GREAT FLAKE TREASURE HUNT

Cadbury's Flake

*FOX'S GLACIER MINTS

' A delicate flavour and smooth in texture' ran the typically
informative but dull strapline for this crystal delicacy when
Leicester's Fox's Confectionery first trumpeted it in 1918. Its equally
dull name, Acme Clear Mint Fingers, was thankfully replaced with
the more poetic Glacier Mints, suggestive of cool refreshment, polar

Opposite: Fox's Glacier Mints (1918),
manufactured by the aptly named Big Bear Ltd
of Braunstone. Oh yes.

45

romance, those heroic British explorers who had so recently frozen to death in the... well, let's just run with the first two for now.

The chilly symbolism worked, though, as the copycat likes of Benson's Arctic Mints attested. But Fox's didn't hang about to be overtaken by the me-too manufacturers. Individual wrappings for the transparent ingots were introduced in 1928, and the brand found a mascot in a moth-eaten stuffed polar bear called Peppy, whose frightening appearance was cleaned up a bit for the labels on the jars.

Peppy was to prove crucial in the mint's '70s resurgence. In June 1972 an unprepossessing series of TV ads was aired, featuring the distinguished, somnolent Peppy (now just called 'Bear') standing proudly on a mint as he had in the logo for so long, while a borderline psychopathic fox ('Fox', if you please) tried various hopeless gambits to dethrone him from his icy perch and reclaim the podium for himself, as was his right, seeing how they were called Fox's mints and that. But, the bear replied in the stately tones of the great Willoughby Goddard, there has to be a bear on the mints because they're 'so cool and clear and min... ty'. This was clearly no kind of answer at all, so Fox kept at it for another twelve years. Then, after a four-year hiatus, he returned, now

having gained a voice himself (albeit one suspiciously similar to Bill Oddie's), but Bear (in an all-new Stratford Johns guise) was as immobile as ever.

Various other products played Fox to Fox's, er, Bear. After the early rash of Arctic This and Polar That, Rowntree's strong, mentholated Lyrics surfaced in 1972, square in shape as opposed to the traditional Fox's ingot but recognisably after its market. They tanked, as did Trebor's 1976 circular hopeful, the Clearmint. That was the problem with clear mints: Bear could see the opposition coming.

Peppy left the 1980s 10 per cent mintier, still in pole position. When a glasnost-initiating Gorbachev mentioned to ICI chairman Sir John Harvey-Jones how his granddaughter loved 'those British mints that look like glass', Sir John had no doubt which brand he meant, and sent him a tin. It's tempting to imagine Gorby crunching a couple himself as he drew up plans for his own, slightly more successful, Fox-vs-Bear act.

*FREDDO

A true star among the largely anonymous chocolate animal milieu, Freddo began life in 1930s Australia when one Harry Melbourne, apprentice chocolate moulder for MacRobertson's, nervously queried his boss's decision to launch a range of choccy mice, suggesting that, as some children (and, of course, all women) were sent into fits of

Opposite: Egg-laying amphibians? Freddo confuses a generation of budding natural historians (circa 1978).

Below: A frog in one's throat? Cadbury's jolly green client (1973).

47

chair-scaling terror at the sight of a rodent, might a frog not be a less risky commercial proposition? Rather than docking him a week's wages for insubordination, Harry's bosses, in a fine example of old-school 'the boy might just be on to something' management, sent him away to knock up a few samples. The resulting amphibian sweetmeat, sporting a cheery countenance and sensible footwear, proved that gut instinct right from the moment it went on sale. When Cadbury took over MacRobertson's it was inevitable that their top-selling line reached the UK.

out, including Freddo soft toys, finger puppets and greetings cards. Then, unaccountably, at the end of the decade he hopped it from British shelves. Perhaps the fame had all become too much. And sure, he's been packing the arenas since his 1994 comeback, but somehow it seems like a soulless, money-raking shadow of former glories. Oh, Freddo, what happened? You used to be all about the chocolate!

Launched in 1973 on a wave of cartoon anthropomorphism and creaky puns about leap years on the wrappers, the British Freddo joined such webbed stars as Kermit, Alberto and the intimidating Grog from *Vision On*, in what turned out to be a singularly froggy decade. By 1974 the lad was turning over £2 million a year. Cadbury's Bournville HQ was inundated with Freddo fan art and fan fiction.

As one exec put it: 'He has a steady band of admirers who enjoy his special brand of humour as well as his eatability.' This estimation was revised upwards the following year to the level of 'national institution', and non-edible merchandise was rolled

*FRY'S FIVE CENTRES

Dark-coated, crescent-shaped and elegant beyond measure, Fry's fondant bars are a product with pedigree. Back in 1853, the Fry brothers boiled up a cauldron of minty fondant and coated strips of it in plain chocolate to make Fry's Chocolate Cream Sticks. In 1866 the 'sticks' fell out of use, some gentle score lines were added for enhanced

Opposite: Centre spread. The changing face of Fry's Five Centres (1934).

49

snappability, and one of Britain's poshest chocolate bars set out on its long life, adverts depicting it in the dainty hands of hat-wearing women of means, often seen buying something dead pricey at an auction, backing a winner at Ascot, or just lounging about being Twiggy.

Well, that's the hat-wearing woman-of-means market sewn up, but what about the kids? In 1934 the first of what would be many incarnations of the more colourful Fry's Five Centres bar came to pass – raspberry, lime, vanilla, coffee and orange fondant centres abutting each other in the plain Chocolate Cream casing. Sadly, the war put this little luxury out of action within a few years.

In 1960 it was reborn. This time the chocolate was a more kid-friendly milk, and the flavours had been slightly altered: now pineapple, raspberry, lime, strawberry and orange centres jostled for position in a new seven-segment bar, the raspberry and strawberry flavours doubling up to fill the gaps. To confuse things further, the wrapper changed design seemingly every year. For a while it was even renamed the Medley. Then in 1982 it vanished again, only to revive, this time back in plain chocolate form, two years later. This final incarnation carried

on until 1992, after which it really was no more.

Despite being rebadged more often than the Austin Metro, one thing remained a familiar constant. No matter how precision-engineered Fry's equipment, the different fondant segments never quite matched up with the dividing grooves in the chocolate shell. Thus a snapped-off chunk might look like pineapple, but the majority turned out to be boring old strawberry. Such intrigue and suspense helped make the Five Centres one of the most fondly recalled sweets of all, even if no two people remember quite the same bar.

*GOLD RUSH

Of all the shapes, sizes, formats and formulae of gum, Bazooka's Gold Rush had to be unique. In an industry where, by and large, bigger is better, this gum's 'small is beautiful' philosophy stood in proud opposition, evidence that even if your product is clearly broken into a hundred tiny pieces, kids will still buy it if it's packaged correctly.

But what a package! The manufacturing process, such as it was, remained shrouded in secrecy but presumably involved large ingots of gum being pulverised into fragments before being sifted from a river bed by thick-'tached Californian prospectors given to cries of 'Yee haw'. And that was just the women. (Ba-dum-tish!) No doubt the end of each shift at the Bazooka factory was marked by much slapping of hats across thighs, shooting of revolvers into the air, fist-fights in the canteen, and so on. It did not matter because Gold Rush's cargo of precious yellow nuggets shipped in its own custom calico fabric bag.

It's difficult to know which is the greater mystery: that no one had considered selling gum with such a USP in the past, or that the drawstring pouch would live on so well in the memory. In a category stuffed with products of zero nutritional value, Gold Rush offered remarkably slim pickings. Available in an uninspired generic fruit flavour (apart from to the Yanks, who also enjoyed raspberry, grape, cherry and 'scented' flavours), its presence in the mouth could go virtually undetected. Any budding Marmalade Atkins attempting to blow a headmaster-baiting bubble would find herself exasperated by the sheer untenable yield in each bagful. Priced at a premium – a pocket-money-sapping 8p in 1978 – the only people striking it rich from Gold Rush were Topps (the Philadelphia-based gum giant) and Trebor (its UK distributors).

At least the triumphant cloth bag proved useful for children to keep other 'treasures' in – a word deliberately employed by the Bazooka sales team but which generally translated into marbles, coins and other such 24-carat crap. A later waterproof version of the bag was also, as it turned out, both consumer- and nostalgia-proof. Countless imitations of the doughty original can be found today but none has staked its claim quite like Gold Rush.

*IPSO

onfectionery may have started as an offshoot of the apothecary's trade, but that doesn't necessarily mean it remains a two-way relationship. Nicholas Laboratories, inventors of Rennie among other mainstays of the bathroom cabinet, found this to their cost when they embarked on a chemically correct assault on the sweet shop in the

Opposite: Calypso lady, shake it down.
Ipso (1979).

53

late 1970s. Things began well enough, with the modest success of Whistling Pops and Sweet Pebbles, irregular gobstoppers bearing an uncanny similarity to ornamental gravel. But to show they meant business they needed a name brand on their books, and for this they looked to the tongue-tingling territory patrolled by the Tic-Tac.

Their carefully formulated riposte, unleashed in orange, mint, raspberry and lemon flavours in 1979, was christened Ipso. Why was never made clear. 'Ipso' is Latin, more or less, for 'itself' (hence the phrase *ipso facto*), a word that's not exactly a harbinger of sugary joy. Perhaps it was coined as a cross-brand bedfellow to Nicholas's Aspro range of headache remedies – but aligning sweets and pills is commercially questionable, to say nothing of potentially dangerous. Equally unfathomable was the choice of packaging: square plastic boxes with bobbles down two adjacent sides which enabled them to join up, LEGO-like, to make various lumpy, two-dimensional shapes in a quaint, yet rather half-arsed, attempt at 'added play value'. Again, the consumer's first question was often: 'Why, exactly?' The packs may have fitted together, but the marketing logic didn't.

Given this blatant appeal to the playful child, it's odd that the TV campaign confused things further, showing the product being scoffed by a businessman, in his suit and tie. Quite rightly avoiding any attempt to represent the Latin tag visually, the ads instead showed a commuter's dull wait for a train enlivened by the refreshing orange sweet, while its idly rattled container sends him into a calypso-based carnival reverie complete with feathered dancers, right there on platform one. Then, just as he starts to loosen up, shed all thoughts of balance sheets and roll his shoulders in classic 'funky duffer' style, he's rudely awoken by a rotund Afro-Caribbean lady (who, one can only surmise, has been tactfully asked by the director to 'be bold' with her ethnicity) with a cheery 'Come on, you'll miss your train!'

Ipsos, it soon transpired, had missed theirs. Maybe it was the cognitive dissonance of the whole enterprise, or maybe the Tic-Tac was just too mighty, but this weird little sweet arrived and departed in a flurry of furrowed young brows and well-meaning racial gaucherie. For the boffins at Nicholas Labs it was back to the stomach pills, their dreams of becoming white-coated Wonkas cruelly crushed.

*JUBBLY

I n the days before Del Boy, and years ahead of Austin Powers (by
way of a plethora of playground ribaldry), Jubbly was nothing
but an innocent drink. Referring to neither bonus nor boobs at the
time, 'luvvly jubbly' (or 'jubblies') was the slogan employed by Sunray
of New Barnet in the 1950s to flog their otherwise ordinary tartrazine-

Opposite: Frozen asset. Jubbly (1950) makes for a nice ice, baby.

Below: Slush Puppie (1977), perpetuating a 'raspberry flavour = blue' ideology in the UK since the *Star Wars* era. 55

tinged offering. The outstanding innovation was in the packaging, an airtight, four-sided, plastic-coated paperboard affair from Swedish design genius Ruben Rausing and his team. The 200ml Tetra Classic debuted in 1958 for milk and non-sparkling drinks and was quickly employed to store and transport Sunray's squash to the nation's shopkeepers. Rumour has it that enterprising proprietors then froze the drinks to prolong their life and sold them on at a penny extra mark-up 'to pay for the electricity'. Snipped at the corner, the triangular blocks of orange ice were sucked and squeezed by little tykes until they turned white.

Despite the immortality conferred on it by John Sullivan's perky Peckham trader, Jubbly was discontinued when Sunray Drinks folded in 1984. A disloyal, disaffected and dehydrated kiddy trade immediately found an alternative – frozen Kwenchy cup drinks from Calypso. These corrugated containers were at least as old as Jubbly and came pre-filled and fitted with a thin film lid. A low price-point ensured that retailers made money hand over fist, and the short incubation period meant any tuck shop entrepreneur could briskly establish their own fruitful icemongery business. The Slush

Puppie arrived on British shores in 1977, swiftly followed by a new phenomenon, 'brain freeze', as kids queued up to chug down a litre or so of cherry or lemon-lime flavour ice crystals in one sitting. Still, nothing quite pushed buttons like the prismatic Jubbly and, sure enough, a tragic tug of love was just around the corner.

Calypso's owners, Cooke Bros of Tattenhall, tried repeatedly to win the rights from Gerber Foods (makers of Libby's fruit drinks), eventually wresting them away after a lamentable TV tie-in with *Gladiators* and a prolonged Patent Office review. In 2005 Jubbly returned to the shelves in its original Tetra-Pak – except, of course, it was considerably smaller than in its 1950s heyday. Even Derek Trotter would have seen through Calypso's slippery PR flim-flam about making it more convenient for junior-sized hands. No amount of retro box-ticking, Chopper bike competition, 'will this do?' promotional activity can excuse it, either. You just can't go around shrinking people's childhood memories – and, for a stone-cold classic like Jubbly, that goes doubly.

*KINDER SURPRISE

The premise was set out in one of this notorious product's many ads. 'What do you want from the shops?' asks Mother, her flashing white teeth and badly dubbed voice indicating she is not of Bermondsey stock. 'Something exciting! And a toy!' reply her equally un-British offspring. 'And some chocolate!' Does she sit them down

Opposite: Kinder Surprise (1974), illegal in the States due to having 'a non-nutritive object imbedded.' Presumably they don't mean the white chocolate.

Below: Buy one, or he will dine on your very soul. Ferrero accidentally commissions Hieronymus Bosch to develop its TV campaign, circa 1984.

57

and give a one-hour lecture on the harsh realities of domestic economics? No. 'But that's three things!' she instead responds, in the unfazed, bubbly laugh of someone who's mixing her prescriptions in cavalier fashion, and merrily trips off to satisfy their exorbitant demands.

The solution comes in the form of Ferrero's happy creation, which arrived on UK soil in 1975: a semi-edible ovoid matryoshka in which a two-tone chocolate shell concealed a Mexican jumping bean-like plastic capsule, which in turn held the pieces of a rudimentary self-assembly plastic toy (always a pirate galleon in the early years, it seemed). It was the archetypal jack-of-all-trades: the chocolate was okay, the toy inevitably ground into the carpet within minutes, and the capsule itself was handy for filling with gravel and throwing at dogs or, for advanced users, gastro-intestinal contraband smuggling.

At first the UK egg market proved hard to crack, thanks mainly to the mighty presence of the Cadbury Creme variety. A steady war of attrition commenced, boosted by unmistakable ads such as the above, and a nightmarish effort that was to live on in the long, dark nights of an entire generation's soul, featuring a boggle-eyed Humpty homunculus speaking in a gobbledegook patter that must have made

Stanley Unwin consultibold his solicitaro. 'Doubly chockadooby!' was the freak's endorsement of the continental treat, only slightly undermined by the qualifying statement, 'Me screwball now!'

Still, it got people looking in Kinder's direction, and the little orange and white critters took their place in a popular culture that was just entering its ironic sweet-mocking middle age. The '90s saw a move away from the generic DIY playthings to a cannily collectable range of anthropomorphic zoological gangs. The Teeny Terrapins, Crazy Crocos, Leoventurers, Happy Hippos and their assorted descendants have filled summer holiday ad breaks with their head-slapping singalong antics ever since. Kinder Surprise: it's a state of mind. Unhinged, to be precise.

*KIT KAT

L aunched around the same time as the Aero, the Rowntree's Chocolate Crisp made much less of a splash. It was just as innovative as its porous counterpart, a chocolate-encased double wafer of the like never seen before. 'The biggest little meal in London' was its original selling point, equating those two snappable fingers to a

Opposite: Golden. Delicious. Kit Kat (1937) celebrates 50 years as a four-fingered favourite.

Below: Eats, shoots and leaves – that Who Dares Wins-indebted panda ad, circa 1989.

59

two-course meal (of, presumably, pudding and pudding). In 1937 it became the Kit Kat Chocolate Crisp, and shortly after the war those last two words were finally dropped. The Kit Kat had arrived.

Problem was, it had arrived pretty much unnoticed. Its humble ambitions – 'the perfect companion to a cup of tea' went the early slogan – hardly marked it out for greatness. Thank heavens, then, for advertising giants J. Walter Thompson, who hatched the 'Have a break' slogan in 1939 and stayed with the bar, and those words, for the rest of the century. Never have three words proved so durable, whether accompanied by Bernard Cribbins as a chatty fisherman, Arthur English as a security guard, or a hapless New Romantic outfit destined to go 'a long way'. In the first half of the '70s, sales rose by over two-thirds on the back of such economical publicity, and seldom faltered afterwards.

Kit Kat statistics make for giddy reading. By 1984, Rowntree were shifting 24 million bars a week. In 1987, forty were said to be eaten every second worldwide. Even so, it never got higher than number two, always the bridesmaid to Mars's bride. Then came Euro expansion: travel to France or Italy in the '80s and you could amaze your school chums by returning with, respectively, five-

and three-fingered mutant Kit Kats.

The rise wasn't inexorable: March 1985 saw the GLC react to Rowntree's lack of transparency regarding disclosure of equal employment opportunities by summarily banning Kit Kats from school tuck shops in the Greater London area. Well intentioned perhaps, but you don't play politics with the kids' lunch, Mr Livingstone. Mrs Thatcher, herself no stranger to snatching dairy produce from the mouths of babes, dissolved the GLC the following year, like a Kit Kat finger in a hot cuppa, just in time for the bar's golden jubilee.

*LOVE HEARTS

Far from being a sweet nothing, a Love Heart always carried a fizzy kick in its compressed sugar make-up; a mixture of tartaric acid and bicarbonate of soda that made it a close relative of powdered sherbet. The chemical reaction when the ingredients were mixed with water (or saliva) created sodium citrate and carbon dioxide, hence the

Opposite: Putting the 'Cor!' into coronary.
Swizzels' much-adored Love Hearts in a none-
too-subliminal 'Buy me' message shocker (1954).

froth and tingling in the mouth. A dry production process (known as 'slugging') had to be enforced to prevent the addition of volatile flavourings and binders from setting off a cannonade of sucrose explosions on the factory floor.

Another of Love Hearts' strengths was the simplicity of the design (a trademarked visual image staunchly defended by the parent company) and its flexibility. The old-fashioned messages appearing on early editions – 1950s' 'Hey, Daddio' – would give way over time to more modern sayings, such as 1960s' 'Gay Boy' or the downright futuristic 'Fax Me'. Even so, they were unlikely to find themselves exchanged for a boy's precious dinner money. Possession equalled intent to supply, and that could only mean one thing: giving a Love Heart to – eurgh! – a girl as a token of affection (after having first carefully arranged the order of the pack – boys were nothing if not as underhand as conjurors forcing cards onto stooges from the audience).

No, it was simply unacceptable. Boys had to have their own version, but it wasn't until 1986 that Swizzels came up with an alternative. Soccer Shields were the result of long and complicated negotiations with the – together at last! – dream team of Southern Television, Manchester Polytechnic and the FA. Each 10p roll came with

a different club sticker from one of the four football league divisions, and a questionnaire about attitudes to the beautiful game (sample: 'If you were in charge of a football club, what would you do to get more people to turn up?'). England team manager Bobby Robson pitched in to plug the survey: leaflets were printed, cardboard cut-outs delivered to newsagents, and some 'Hey kids!' speech-bubble-friendly quotes sourced, all featuring the white-haired World Cup wizard.

However, Robson bowed out after a single appearance on flagging Saturday morning children's TV show, *Number 73*, and was replaced by last-minute substitution 'Big Ron' Atkinson (who was presumably pleased to note that the packets didn't contain any 'lazy, thick' black ones). The glamorous football associations belied the fact that Soccer Shields, available in either 'mint' or 'refresher' varieties, were a partial reinvention of 1972's Lucky Strike, 'the sweet that won £250,000 on the pools'. Dads were encouraged to use

these as counters to help choose the score draws for their Treble Chance each Saturday, although Swizzels also gave away plenty of Lunn Poly holidays and Hillman Avengers via a more traditional 'write a slogan' competition.

Soccer Shields' time in the top flight was brief. On paper, the lads gave 110 per cent but, at the end of the day, it was just end-to-end stuff. Love Hearts continued to lead the field, boosted by the occasional headline (a lorryload of 3 million packs nicked and recovered in 1973) or royal endorsement (a factory visit by Princess Di in 1990). What no one could have predicted was the personalised wedding favours produced for the nation's sweethearts, Wayne and Colleen Rooney, in 2008. Confectionery – it's a funny old game, isn't it?

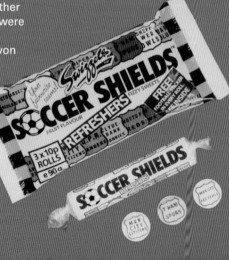

*MARS

Jargon alert! Ask any chocolatier (and who doesn't know at least three?) and they will tell you: a substantial majority of their profits is generated by 'countlines', those smooth choc-covered treats, filled with nougat, caramel, ill-fated factory-floor rats and so on, designed to be eaten on the move.

Opposite: The cash cow of Slough: Mars (1932) and the slogan that first appeared in print in 1959

Below: If you can't run one, eat one. Marathon (1968).

65

This particular form of one-handed pleasure isn't easy to sell. Before the days of commercial television, kids were too busy up chimneys and picking pockets to buy their own sweets. The advent of advertising brought increasingly ingenious campaigns to remind us that countlines were reliable, dependable and enjoyable.

So, when Mars brought their popular candy bar over from the US to London in 1932, deliberately changing the recipe to suit European tastes (more sugar, less malt, sweeter caramel and, at first – unbelievably – Cadbury's chocolate), they were unwittingly helping a future slogan-writer (not Murray Walker, despite what you might read elsewhere) come over all expert practitioner: 'A Mars a day helps you work, rest and play'. TV screens could be filled with sumptuous close-ups of sugar, caramel and thick, thick chocolate slathering over a nougat slab, yet still reinforce the impression that the Mars bar was not only nutritious, but practically vital.

Marathon, on the other hand, was positioned firmly as a meal replacement: 'packed with peanuts', curbing and satisfying hunger pangs like a chocolate dominatrix. 1970s ads featured the bar itself repeatedly disassembling into slices before Keith Chegwin's startled eyes. This inspired parents to carve up and share out a single bar among siblings, each of whom would fight tooth and claw to be allocated a chocolate-heavy end piece.

Ever alert to consumer behaviour, Mars's product developers speedily introduced the fun-size bar. From 1972 onward, everyone could have their own end piece. Pound for pound, they were more expensive than their standard-sized counterparts, but such is the marketeer's sleight of hand. To allay mums' housekeeping money fears, some friendly adverts demonstrated how much more a bag-load weighed than a box of posh chocs. 'Two bites big,' they said. Big! Not small. The scales couldn't lie.

In 1989, Marathon began to carry little 'internationally known as' badges (soon swapped for 'the new name for') as Snickers' dominance asserted itself. 'All that's changed is the name' bleated the label, as if that were a mere trifle. A new recipe had never been on the cards, but it was a handy distraction from the fact that Snickers was, and is, a ghastly name.

*MILKY BAR

Though pre-dating Alan Parker's much admired all-juvenile *Bugsy Malone* casting policy by some two decades, the Milky Bar ads were surely made by marketing men both short on imagination and long on memory. A few short scenes were recycled and remade every few years for a new generation of chocoholic tots. To the tune of

Opposite: Milky Bars (1937) featuring the whip-crackaway whippersnapper himself. No sign of Big Chief Milky Bar, introduced in 1977 'for ethnic balance'.

Below: The return of the space cowboy. The Milky Bar Kid faces the final frontier, and some unconvincing aliens, in a telly ad circa 1982.

67

a honky-tonk saloon bar piano, and the repetitive mantra of the titular song's rhyming couplets, the 'strong and tough' Milky Bar kid would save faux Frontiersmen from some minor inconvenience or other before declaring, 'The Milky Bars are on me,' at which point a cheering crowd of sugar-crazed urchins would surge forward to grab the proffered treats.

That said, this was not chocolate as any British child had experienced it before, largely comprising cocoa butter (without the requisite powder), milk solids and vanilla, stretched out into a waxy, sugary tablet. Whiffing faintly of distant Common Market subsidies, it could appeal only to the most immature of tastes; the creamiest milk, maybe, but the plasticiniest bar by far. Inevitably, the Milky Bar kid himself was as puny and pallid as the product he was paid to endorse, all alabaster skin and wire-rimmed specs, though eternally youthful thanks to a sequence of lead actor changes that would put *Doctor Who* to shame. The fortunes of each much heralded gunslinger would wane as the voice broke, the freckles faded and puberty inflicted an inescapable and implacable grip on his hormonal system. Cue the difficult transition back to normal life and a future career in loft conversion, panel beating or haulage, alongside the perennial tabloid 'off the rails' headlines. For the most

unfortunate, that early, illusive taste of fame was as much a curse as a blessing.

Meanwhile, the campaign rolled on with such bandwagon-jumping anachronisms as 'the Milky Bar kid out in space' (defeating evil green overlord Zartan with a laser-deflecting silver platter) and 1987's circus-themed Buttons launch, though quite what recondite career path led the Milky Bar kid from cowboy to big top ringmaster went unremarked upon.

*PACERS

W hy did they used to put so many vending machines in sport and leisure centres? Well, for the cash, obviously, but also 'cos those crafty confectioners wanted to link consumption of their yummy, energy-packed products with an active, healthy lifestyle. In 1975, when doing a few widths of the shallow end, skipping the showers and spending the rest of a Saturday morning stinking of chlorine and nicotine in the smokers' gallery put a kid right up there with David Wilkie, liberating a packet of sweets from behind D7 wasn't going to do anyone any harm. The creeping emphysema could be staved off with a sugar rush.

Hence, Pacers: the Adidas of soft minty chews. Originally just plain old Opal Mints, they gained a new name and exciting peppermint stripes around the time Team GB won gold in the 200 metres breast stroke at the Montreal Olympics. The sporty allusions were rife: on TV, perma-grinning ice-dancers, goalkeepers and roller-skaters saw their pristine, Daz-white kit graffitied with a green three-bar motif 'to give a two-mint freshness'. And, as even the spoddiest, drawstring-Day-Glo-pump-bag-carrying dork at the swimming baths knew, stripes seriously improved the coolness factor. It's why Bodie and Doyle ditched their clunky British Leyland cars for go-faster Ford Capris. It's why Signal was more fun to clean your teeth with than Gibbs SR. It's why Pepé Le Pew's girlfriends got some action.

But why add them to Pacers? Was it simply because Mars, suffering a touch of the Steve Austins, discovered that they had the technology? Or was it to bring them in line with the identical American candy of the same name? Prior to stripification, each carefully sealed wax paper wrapper contained a square, emulsified chunk of vegetable fat and glucose the exact colour and consistency of a church candle. Any such religious connotation, sensibly, was disregarded by the marketing bods. No one wanted to see impressionable Catholic kids gnawing on tea-lights during the liturgy. However, in upgrading to an improved two-tone pattern, Mars may have caused a schism amid the football faithful of Glasgow. Celtic supporters could wield a chew kitted out in their home strip, whereas partisan Rangers fans would be less inclined to partake.

It mattered not. Enthusiastically advertised or otherwise, Pacers wheezed asthmatically into the '80s before collapsing in an armchair of obscurity. Their name has passed into history. Optimistic Googlers will find only a list of increasingly provincial running clubs and Indiana-based basketball teams. The health Nazis won: fitness centre vending machines are now full of fruit and Mini Babybels. Now those really do taste like wax.

*PICNIC

S o, you've got your basic filled bar: an inner core of some stout substance (biscuit, nougat, toffee) covered in chocolate. To jazz it up, you can stick stuff to the outside. Nuts. Raisins. Rice. Cornflakes. Do that, and you've got one of the family of odd-shaped chocolate bars that aren't, but perhaps should be, known collectively as 'the knobblies'.

Opposite: Raisin 'arris owner. The changing face of Cadbury's Picnic (1958)

Below: Wild thing. Lion Bar (1976), originally 71 designed by Rowntree's Allan Norman.

The family has its origins in the venerable, if slightly lumpy, shape of the Rowntree's Nux. Seven long years in development, what started as a chewy chocolate bar laced with peanuts and raisins finally surfaced in shops in 1957 coated in hazelnuts and Rice Krispies. The extended gestation period, sadly, didn't prepare it for the harsh realities of the 1960s snack market, and it finally passed on in 1965.

Chief among its reasons for collapse was the Fry's Picnic, which appeared in 1958. This went for a peanut and raisin combo, but built it around a sturdy caramel wafer chassis, and dolloped a generous amount of Cadbury's milk chocolate over the whole shebang. Later came the addition of the inevitable puffed rice to the mix, bringing it closer to its stablemate from 1963 onwards, Mackintosh's Toffee Crisp.

Then things got confusing. In 1972 Mackintosh launched the Prize, which aped the Picnic's peanut and raisin coating, but applied it instead to a core of fudge. This they brought out at exactly the same time sister company Rowntree unleashed the Nutty, which was what you got if you

took a Prize, removed the raisins and chocolate, injected it with caramel and wrapped it in transparent brown cellophane. And if you did that, you deserved what you got.

Then five years later they were at it again. Rowntree's Lion Bar was, to all intents and purposes, one scoop of peanuts short of a Picnic, but instead of going for the wacky branding angle, respectable wrappers and ads showing noble beasts in majestic repose gave the knobbly genre an altogether classier, more adult image.

Licking its wounds, the beast of Bournville retired to its laboratory, leaving the knobbly market in a steady state. Then, in 1985, Cadbury unveiled the Boost, a log of coconut and caramel, swiftly joined by biscuit and peanut variants, which cleverly purloined the ancient Mars bar tenet: 'It's absolutely packed full of sugar therefore it'll have you bouncing off the walls – but in an entirely productive fashion.'

*POLO

You always hear about the nylons and the chewing gum. And the first tantalising glimpses of an aspirational, can-do lifestyle hitherto alien to these islands. And shagging round the back of the NAAFI wagon. But what did those American GIs really do for us? They brought us the Polo. It was properly called the Lifesaver, but during the

Opposite: Tubular sells: the familiar marque o' Polo (1948) and Polo Fruits (1953).

Below: Nobody does it better. TV advertising, that is, circa 1986.

73

war Rowntree were granted the licence from their manufacturer to make them over here especially for homesick Yanks. After VE Day, a canny bit of tweaking resulted in Rowntree's own version, initially called Pax but soon renamed Polo Digestive Mints. It wasn't an easy start. The 'digestive' moniker was hastily withdrawn when Rowntree were challenged to prove the sweet's medicinal credentials. Then they had to see off a number of copycat rivals like Swizzels' Navy Mints. But by the '50s the Polo had established itself as one of the top 'motoring mints' in town, thanks to its resilient constitution and that hole, which maximised the surface area through which the sucker's tongue could extract mintiness.

When you've got the perfect formula, what else to do but muck about with it? Typically for Americans, Life Savers came in all sorts of cockamamie flavours from violet to malted milk. Things were more restrained over here. Plans were made for barley sugar Polos, and a Glacier Mint-baiting crystal clear variety, but nothing came of them. Polo Fruits, however, did trundle shelfwards in 1953, the familiar foil tube replaced by waxed paper, within which hard, semi-opaque and very, very sticky fruit sweets clung together as if for dear life. Such tactics were futile: if you couldn't prise a group of three apart, you did the honourable thing and downed it in one. (Later variants, like lemon

and the short-lived strawberries and cream flavour, stuck to the non-stick format of the originals.)

Despite 'the Mint with the Hole's reputation as a Sunday driver's companion (Rowntree offered free holiday route maps in one giveaway), two-thirds of consumers were women. Predictably, this led to a scare about the mint somehow cancelling out the effects of the Pill. Nothing, though, could sway it from its steady-as-she-goes residency at the top of the minted pops: least of all half-arsed 1981 rival Meltis Mints, a Trebor clone whose centre dissolved faster in the mouth than the rest, turning it into a Polo clone mid-suck. No takers. Meanwhile, a series of wry minimalist ads voiced by Peter Sallis (a pair of sturdy driving gloves in audio form) kept the Polo firmly within the Zeitgeist, and that little well next to the gear stick, without actually changing a thing.

From Rowntrees with love.

*REESE'S PIECES

If you asked any British kid in 1982 what E.T.'s favourite sweets were the chances are they'd tell you they weren't allowed to talk to strangers and run off. Hooray! Those public information films weren't a total waste of money, then. But ask the same question in the States and you'd receive an ebullient reply: 'Reese's Pieces!'

Opposite: Exquisite. Exotic. Extra-terrestrial. Reese's Pieces (1978), arguably the first truly intergalactic product placement.

Below: Rich E.T. biscuits. Britain's altogether more urbane take on the 'phone home' phenomenon (1983).

75

Spielberg's interstellar goblin conquered cinemas and hearts clutching a handful of Hershey's own peanut butter 'candies', though they would remain unknowable to the UK until 1996.

To add to the confusion, William Kotzwinkle's novelisation of the film was worked up from an older draft of the screenplay and so made prominent mention of M&Ms (which, themselves, wouldn't debut in Britain's sweet shops proper until the late '80s), because it was originally intended that the bug-eyed gastronaut would chomp on those instead. Oh, for want of 'find and replace', eh, Bill? It's a small inconsistency but one that throws some light on a huge behind-the-scenes battle for supremacy in the market for tiny chocolate beans.

But who copied whom? Forrest Mars had originally taken his proposition to the Hershey factory and, while he couldn't convince the company to buy his idea, soon bagged himself a business partner in R. Bruce Murrie, son of the then president. With borrowed machinery and a contract to supply American GIs with bags of the candies for war rations, production began in 1940 on their eponymous M&Ms. Murrie, not having much of a

taste for the chocolate industry, didn't stick around for long, though his initial lives on. Hershey-Ets were M&Ms' nearest rival, though ironically not in the eyes of the Extra-Terrestrial, who favoured the 'peanuche' middle of Reese's Pieces. Mars, of course, had turned down the opportunity to be associated with the all-conquering alien and famously lost out on a killer product placement deal. It later transpired that Jack Dowd, marketing manager for Hershey, had signed the contract with Universal Pictures sight unseen and had no idea how ugly the creature was until it was unveiled at a private screening for his staff much later. Though, after trebling sales in a matter of weeks off the back of the movie's endorsement, it's no surprise that Hershey bosses were happy to go on record as saying E.T. was quite, quite beautiful.

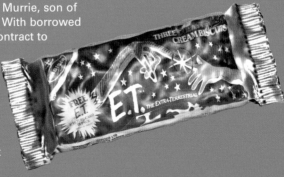

*REVELS

I n the confectionery business, you're onto a winner if you can give the impression of offering more for less, and Mars took that precept to the limit with Revels, which must have been the cheapest product to launch in sweet-making history. After all, Maltesers and Galaxy Counters were already going, and the peanut and toffee varieties would

Opposite: Let the revels commence! Mars's motley medley (1967)

Below: Bags more for everyone? Bagsy those uneaten chocs, more like. TV ad, circa 1978.

77

be recycled as Treets a few years later. The only 'true' Revels were the coconut and orange (later coffee) cream-centred chocs, which, perhaps tellingly, are the ones that compete for status of 'most hated flavour' in folk mythology.

The thriftiness extended to the advertising campaigns, with cheeky newsagents admonishing, 'You can't buy a box of chocolates for sixpence, sonny!' Post-decimalisation, the comparison was eked out in a recession-busting commercial wherein a half-pound bag of Revels was poured into an empty chocolate box, filling it to the brim in a most satisfying way. (The inconvenient truth that boxes of chocolates have always been pretty rotten value for money was tactfully ignored.)

As well as the impression of abundance on the cheap, Revels got into the underage public consciousness via the many opportunities their multifarious nature offered for juvenile mucking about (for kids, food you can fart about with invariably sits higher up the cultural pecking order than food that's only good for stuffing in your gob). Peanut-allergic comedian Milton Jones reminisced about school bullies forcing him to play Russian roulette with a bag in the playground, a gag which Mars, thrifty to the last, 'borrowed' for a *Deer Hunter*-parodying ad in 2002. You can't buy an ad campaign for sixpence, sonny...

*ROLO

Romance and chocolate have always walked hand in hand, like a pair of soppy-gobbed love-muffins. They speak a common language, all sweetness this, sugar that, and syrupy the other. Maybe it's the Freudian link between the filling the mouth and giving pleasure. Maybe it's the oft-identified, though scientifically disputed,

Opposite: Rolo (1937), marketed as 'a chocolate cup-o-toffee' circa 1972. Which is an improvement on 'a chocolate conical frustum'. But less geometrically accurate.

79

chemical mix of theobromide and phenylethylamine (the 'love drug'). Certainly, even Casanova himself was said to partake of a bite or two prior to bedding his conquests. Whatever the truth, it's a relationship advocated by chocolatiers – as any spotty teenager trying to impress the object of his or her affections has learned over time.

Chief among the culprits is the otherwise unassuming Rolo, forged in an auspicious union of 'soft, chewy toffee in a milk chocolate cup' by Caley-Mackintosh. The two companies had themselves entered into a marriage of convenience in 1932 which meant Halifax's self-proclaimed Toffee King no longer had to rely solely on butter and molasses products to turn a pretty, gold-foiled penny. Bite-sized, chocolate-coated creations rolled off the drawing board and into the sweaty paws of lovestruck youth. Rolo was the entry-level brand, joined in 1955 by the cool and cultivated, plain chocolate Mintola (at the time, identical in size and shape to its older brother), and shortly after by radically square biscuit luxury, Munchies. All were packaged in 'the perfect pocket pack' to encourage sharing, that pre-Internet equivalent of viral marketing, and thus commenced many a back-row courtship under dimmed cinema lights.

Only a quarter of a century later did anyone back at HQ think to make use of the amorous association. Late '60s 'Rolo Sensation' adverts made brief stars of Danish kazoo-and-comb rockers Sir Henry and His Butlers and their international hit, 'Camp'. But it was on the back of their 'Do you love anyone enough to give them your last?' campaign that Rolo truly tugged at the nation's heartstrings. In 1986 the selfish-seeming Large Rolo was quietly withdrawn, and an extra 'last' Rolo was added to standard-sized tubes. A successful series of animations featured an existential young suitor who became increasingly self-aware as he was illustrated on the page, bashfully offering his final toffee to a beautifully drawn girl. Saatchi and Saatchi even pulled a stunt, placing appropriately painted Rolo posters along the route of Prince Andrew and Sarah Ferguson's royal wedding.

Munchies and Mintola meanwhile were left behind. An attempt to broaden the range with Rum Truffles, Wholenut in caramel and you-know-what-ish Delights failed. Rolo even trumped their rare opulence with a boxed, solid silver incarnation intended for Valentine's Day gifting (not for consumption), although Fergie probably does chomp her way through a fair number of these. Hence all those money worries.

*ROWNTREE'S FRUIT GUMS AND PASTILLES

Descendants of the medicated throat sweet, the fruit gum and fruit pastille were perfected by Rowntree, living testimonies to the power of direct marketing. Both the hard, jewel-like gums and their softer, sugar-encrusted colleagues had been available for decades,

Opposite: Fruit deuce. Rowntree's enduring Fruit Gums (1893) and Fruit Pastilles (1881).

Below: Love you lots like Jelly Tots (1965). 81 Sweet precursor to the since-extinct Tiger, Candy and Bunny (later Teddy) Tots.

sold loose in paper bagfuls scooped from traditional jars, but in 1938 Rowntree stuck them in handy foil and paper tubes festooned with their corporate livery.

The effect of this move was twofold. First the tubes became more of an impulse buy, thus competing with new big-name chocolate products like the Mars bar. In addition, the sweets were packaged in a permanent advertisement for their manufacturers. Every time you reached for a pastille, there was Rowntree's, bold as brass. Other companies made almost identical sweets, but whose brand would you remember? The one you glimpsed over the grocer's shoulder, or the one that spent all day in your back pocket?

Spin-offs abounded. Butterscotch and liquorice gums were (thankfully) short-stay varieties in 1960, but junior pastille variant Jelly Tots established itself in 1965, and a tube full of the most popular flavour, blackcurrant, did well enough to achieve sitcom immortality when Tony Hancock advised Hugh Lloyd, 'They do a tube with all black ones now, you know.'

An early ITV campaign in which a snotty kid chanted 'Don't forget the Fruit Gums, Mum' gave rise to complaints of copycat irritation. Rowntree's molar-hugging oral longevity was trumpeted in a new wave of ads, from the Fruit Gum-fuelled antics of Sir Lastalot and Ye Knights of Ye Rowntree's Table to a perennially unimpressed child who greeted various feats of skill with the rejoinder 'Not bad, but I bet you can't put a Rowntree's Fruit Pastille in your mouth without chewing it.' Most elaborate of all was 1982's Fruit Gums Secret – a series of cryptic posters given away in comics providing clues to a postal address, which, if worked out and contacted, would garner the lucky winner the unusual prize of a time-share villa. Forget Frisbees and pencil cases, this was aspirational stuff.

These sweets were loved through good times and bad. Idiosyncrasies were forgiven, even cherished, like the way the gums tended to stick to each other, raising questions of etiquette when one person offered another a single gum, only to part company with several at once. A late '80s change to a less sticky, more wine-gummy consistency made ergonomic sense, but were Rowntree thanked? Nope, they just got stick for screwing with a classic recipe. Fickle folk, chewers.

*SHERBET FOUNTAIN

When Tangerine, the Blackpool-based owners of Sherbet Fountain, updated the sweet's packaging in 2009, they faced a perfect storm of media outrage. 'A step too far,' seethed the *Independent*. 'Killjoys,' moaned the *Daily Mail*. 'Annoying,' fumed the *Guardian*. It was all rather predictable, given Fleet Street's known

Opposite: Memoirs of a geyser. Barratt's
Sherbet Fountain (1925).

83

aversion to change and
bloodhound's nose for stories that
might rile the proletariat. 'Hygiene'
was the self-confessedly anaemic
reason Tangerine gave for the
plastic makeover, though deaths
attributed to virulent liquorice or
toxic sherbet had been few and
far between over the preceding
eighty-odd years.

The new, hermetically sealed
Sherbet Fountain genuinely did
fix some flaws: it protected the
product from moisture, avoided
spillage on newsagents' shelves
and prevented sabotage. But
– from the Just Williams to the
Adrian Moles – generations of
wilful kids had delighted in its
original, eccentric form. Tucked
in the back pocket, along with
a catapult or a secret diary,
that yellow paper tube looked
pleasingly like a stick of dynamite
or a (potentially name-coining)
firework. Unpacked, the useless
treacly liquorice 'straw' could
be quickly dispatched and full
attention directed to the contents
within. If the weather was fine,
this would most likely result in an
explosion of dusty lemon sherbet
and a day condemned to walk
the streets with a pierrot-white
face. If wet, the porous cardboard
would dampen like a tramp's roll-
up, causing the sherbet to stick
to the sides in claggy lumps and
necessitating a lean-back and
open-wide manoeuvre. Squeezing
and tapping a fully loaded Sherbet
Fountain into your mouth carried

with it the risk, at the very least, of
a full-on coughing fit.

Here's where the modernisers
went wrong. You can add as much
anti-caking agent as you like, but
take away that sense of danger
and you subtract from the overall
eating experience. Ironing out the
wrinkles and streamlining defects
might make sense on the factory
floor, but what made the Sherbet
Fountain so endearing was its
essential Britishness: it was tactile,
an action sweet, but nothing
about it worked as it ought to. Like
Morecambe and Wise sharing a
big double bed, it sort of looked
wrong, but it sort of felt right.

Barratt themselves had previously
experimented with the formula,
inflicting orange and raspberry
varieties on an ungrateful public.
In 1995, Monkhill also tried to
tempt the nation into supping
the Sherbet Fountain in soda
drink form. Yet nothing scared the
horses like plastic-gate, which
was strange, because – in among
all the hand-wringing over the
less recyclable nature of the new
tube – no one spotted that the
flavour of the sherbet had also
changed. Now, that one really
should have had the journalists
foaming at the mouth.

*SMARTIES

I n common with most British confectioners of the nineteenth century, Henry Isaac Rowntree, cocoa merchant and denizen of York society, also acquired and published a newspaper. Preoccupied thereafter with matters of the fourth estate, he decided, in 1881, to entrust his brother, the philanthropist and social reformer Joseph Rowntree, with

Opposite: 'How many tubes would it take to go round the Underground?' Only Smarties (1937) have the answer.

Below: Bean feast. Smarties Eggheads are a hollow victory, circa 1977.

85

building a new chocolate factory. The first new products to roll off the conveyor belt twelve months later were small, colourful beans modelled on French dragées, sold loosely in bags to little tykes and bigwigs alike. Unfortunately, Henry died within a year, while Joseph's business went from strength to strength; proof if any were needed that chocolate is good for you, whereas journalism can be fatal.

Fast-forward to 1937 (the peak of snack food's very own age of light and innovation) and the beans were now being packaged in cardboard tubes and familiarly trademarked as Smarties (in the UK only, short-sightedly letting an American candy maker hijack the name across the Atlantic). Skip forward again, to 1959, and someone had the bright idea of introducing a plastic cap with a random letter of the alphabet on as 'an attractive plaything for children'. Strangely, the nation's letters to Santa that Christmas still resolutely favoured Barbie, Frisbees and Sea Monkeys. The real stroke of genius was taking out the disgusting coffee-flavoured ones the year before: take note, Revels.

In the following decades, a generation of swinging '60s kids learned to 'buy some for Lulu', while the hyperactive, multicultural, singing and dancing 'Smarties scene' did for the '70s (at least until the International

Trade Group insisted on the removal of the phrase 'chocolate beans' in order to avoid confusing those few French people who were spoiling their cassoulets). In the '80s, Rowntree threw in their lot with the British National Book League to offer the Smarties Prize for Children's Literature (igniting another 'is it all right to rot your teeth, as long as you're expanding your mind?' ethical debate among metropolitan middle-class commentators). Monster-sized tubes, square sharing boxes, Easter eggs (and Eggheads) all made an appearance, as did hyperactive, multi-channel, singing and dancing CGI adverts courtesy of top pixel-wranglers Robinson Lambie-Nairn. Then, as the '90s dawned, not long after the introduction of blue Smarties, the ultimate tribute: a rubbish chart hit by a rave outfit styling themselves 'the Smart E's'. The similarity between Henry Isaac's chocolate beans and house music's disco biscuits has often been questioned, particularly by the tabloid press he'd so keenly wanted to be part of. It just goes to show: chocolate can be good for you, but techno is fatal.

*SPACE DUST

L ike *Star Wars*, the Sony Walkman and serial killers, this fizzy sherbet sensation was a huge hit in the States long before the Brits got their tiny mitts on it. US confectionery giant General Foods had been sitting on a patent for a process to introduce pressurised gas into candy for nigh on twenty years. It took until 1976 for the manufacturing capability to

Opposite: Space Dust (1977). Or, as the picture might suggest, Moon Puke. (Wasn't she one of Frank Zappa's kids?)

87

catch up with the conjecture, at which point Pop Rocks – the first of their kind – literally exploded onto the market.

Demand, however, quickly outstripped supply. Tiny black envelopes of the stuff changed hands in New York City playgrounds at a higher price by weight than the kind of white lines Grandmaster Flash sang dang diggedy dang di-dang about. Like their street drug counterparts, Pop Rocks also attracted a fair share of newspaper scare stories. Rumours spread that kids who quaffed a can of Coke and chugged three packs at the same time could suffer from what top physicians call 'exploding stomach syndrome', despite daily evidence to the contrary. The urban legend was so tenacious that General Foods felt compelled to send their top food scientist, William A. Mitchell, on a coast-to-coast, myth-busting tour. Even so, consumer resistance coupled with persistent distributor bootlegging did for sales and the company faced a $34 million loss on the product.

Their second attempt was Space Dust, the budgie grit to Pop Rocks' fish tank gravel. Less startling than the original, being more tongue-corroding than tooth-cracking, it sparkled in orange, grape and watermelon flavours for the Yanks, or 'orbiting' orange, 'solar' strawberry and 'lunar' lemon for the Limeys. Nevertheless, the stench of scandal followed, leading Britain's Ministry of Agriculture to investigate unsourced reports that Space Dust gave you cancer (it didn't) and the tabloids to claim that grown-ups were using it to spike their beer (they weren't). General Foods, already spooked, changed the name to Cosmic Candy back home (to avoid further unwanted comparisons with Angel Dust), while the UK launch of Pop Rocks misfired like a mouth-bound blunderbuss. No amount of free 'I'm a Pop Rocker' badges could make it sound less like a stale mid-'70s ITV music show for teens. It was all over. In 1983, Chris Kelly and co. documented the demise of such space-age sweetdom on the Beeb's *Food & Drink* programme.

Not that they ever really went away: by the late '80s Hannah's of Johnstone had already begun importing Peta Zetas popping candy from Spain under the name Fizz Wiz. In the '90s, Duncan's of Scotland were granted exclusive use of the Space Dust trademark to power their Shock-A-Lot choc bar. Yet, despite the fact that a quick Google Shopping search instantly reveals at least half a dozen different brands still on sale, a belief in this sweet's scarcity persists. Consequently, a nostalgia-baiting TV chef can sprinkle a pack on his dessert to wow ingenuous C-list celebrity guests and be declared a retro genius. Oh yeah? Well, knock us up a giant pack of Spangles, Heston, and maybe we can talk.

*SPANGLES

The year is 1948, and the world is rebuilding itself from the most catastrophic conflict of modern times, filling the void of civilisation with equal amounts of optimism and despair. In the latter camp, George Orwell writes *1984*, a nightmare vision of an omnipotent totalitarian regime. On a lighter note, Mars's Slough factories thrum to the production

Opposite: The sweet, sweet taste of industrial action – take a trip back in time to the 1970s with Spangles (er, 1948).

89

of new 'luscious assorted crystal fruits': Spangles. Little does either party know how culturally ingrained both items would become.

Just as 'It's like 1984' has become a cliché when talking about institutional repression, 'Remember Spangles?' is the nationally recognised catchphrase of corny nostalgia. Why this particular, innocuous rectangle of boiled sugar, moulded with fingertip-friendly indentations ('the dimple in the Spangle takes your tongue straight to the heart of the flavour!'), should have been singled out is unclear. Two generations of baby boomers happily crunched them without much fuss. They were rather nice boiled sweets, advertised with none-more-whimsical rhymes ('Farmers love Spangles!/Charmers love Spangles!/Nice little boys in pyjamas love Spangles!') and that was that.

The thing is, Spangles were nostalgic even back then. Despite those innovative foil tubes, they harked unashamedly back to the pre-war days of the sweet shop staffed by a cheery man in front of an endless array of big glass jars. 'Enjoy your favourite jar sweets the modern Spangles way!' The '50s and '60s saw a plethora of new varieties: butterscotch, liquorice, glucose barley sugar, golden mint, soft centre ice mint, the infamous herbally infused Old English assortment, and even a 'mystery flavour' with a question-mark-studded wrapper. In 1974, when that lost its shine, modernisation was the thing: a groovy bell-bottomed typeface, 'fizzy' flavours (lemonade, orangeade and cola) and a Day-Glo TV ad in which a juvenile Nicholas Lyndhurst and pals cavorted in a lido with giant berries. ('Suck a Spangle – get happy!')

Ironically, it was this final incarnation that would stick. Never mind the three decades' worth of post-war sucking, after Mars discontinued the Spangle (spookily enough, in 1984), their final incarnation joined space hoppers and power cuts in the dressing-up box of default 1970s ephemera.

In 1994 Spangle nostalgia ate itself when Woolworth's assisted in a relaunch of the tangerine, lime, blackcurrant and Old English flavours as a limited edition reminisci-snack, promoted with woolly nostalgia pieces in the popular press, and Honor Blackman draped over the bonnet of an E-Type Jag. The revamp didn't last, but the cliché did. Eventually the passage of time will see off all surviving Spangle-era veterans, and the topic will be confined to the history books. But if you want a vision of the foreseeable future, imagine a human face going 'Spangles? What were all that about?!' forever.

*TERRY'S ALL GOLD

Though for years your bog-standard half-pound box o' chocs had been sold primarily to chivalrous, guilty or desperate men, never had the boat been pushed out further than by Terry's All Gold. Buying was no longer an act of obligation, it was about responding to a modern woman desirous of opulence and an altogether better class of

Opposite: 'Alchemy! Alchemy! They've all got it alch...' No, that doesn't work. Terry's All Gold (1932).

Below: An admission of gilt? The posh chocolate payoff, circa 1982.

91

chocolate. Just reading the names of the individual sweetmeats was an exercise in extravagance: Honeycomb Jewel, Russian Caramel, Chartreuse Bullion. The words themselves rolled around on the tongue long before the cocoa butter, invert sugar syrup and soya lecithin.

A cosmopolitan – some might say ecumenical – selection nestled in among the various kegs, ingots and clusters as were found in lesser assortments. No pick 'n' mix, this. If anything, Terry's All Gold aspired to exclusivity, conjuring up allusions to bespoke art collections, haute couture pieces, eclectic jeweller's windows... or some such other pretentious guff. The long-running ads only served to reinforce the sense of heritage, entitlement and implicit worth of the product. An upper-crust crooner of the Peter Skellern school entreated the viewer to 'see the face you love light up' as a porcelain-skinned chatelaine in an emerald organza dress ran lacquered fingernails across the box lid. Her tuxedo-clad beau remained at a respectful distance, half in shadow, confident in the knowledge he'd eventually be called upon to eat the one with the brazil nut in it. (The literal 'lighting up' of the loved one's face, a muted cascade of candlelight bouncing off metallic embossed cardboard, was an effect undoubtedly pinched wholesale by Quentin Tarantino

for *Pulp Fiction*. What's in the mysteriously dazzling briefcase? Is it Marcellus Wallace's soul? No. It's the Lemon Barrel.)

Never more than in the acquisitive '80s, with its Spandau Ballet records, futures trading and Leeds Building Society savings accounts, was gold so much a symbol of ostentatious elitism and luxury. Nowadays, platinum is the new standard, but that's inflation for you. The phrase Terry's All Gold, on the other hand, has been relegated to the back pages of tabloid newspapers for use as a cheap headline about footballers. (Footballers called Terry, usually. That's how tabloids work.)

*TEXAN

The history of British sweets marketed by knock-off cowboys is long and baffling. When the Milky Bar kid first flaunted the only NHS prescription in nineteenth-century Nevada, kids did indeed still flock to the flicks for historically dubious tales of ethnic cleansing in fetching hats. By the time Rowntree Mackintosh launched their Mighty

Opposite: Rowntree's much-missed Lone Star bar, Texan (1973).

Below: Rope 'em in. Move 'em out. Eat 'em up. TV's ten-gallon toffee-lover, circa 1977.

93

Chew on the knee-high populace, however, the predominant Western image was of Gran dozing off in front of *The High Chaparral*.

Nevertheless, in the strong, silent, jaw-jutting mould of Eastwood and Wayne, the Texan Man was effective enough. But whereas Nestlé's bespectacled law enforcer was an Aryan-tressed riot of six-shooting roundup action, our cartoon friend's capabilities were limited to getting caught by a variety of racial stereotypes. Injuns and Mexicans alike tied him up, frugged wildly about, then foolishly granted him a last request: a chance to scoff his Texan bar. The resulting postponement of atrocities via the prolonged mastication of chocolate and nougatine eventually rendered his foes unconscious, whereupon he would untie himself, tiptoe over his dozing captors, and mooch off to bore the crap out of some other ethnic minority. He livened up in later ads, effecting daring escapes from ice floes and stagecoaches, and even performed a rather lasciviously chocophiliac hoedown ('Take your Texan by the hand/Strip it down! My, that's grand!'), but mainly it was a case of trudging about, sending foreigners to sleep and being, by cowboy standards, a bit of a useless arse.

Not that any of this dented the success of the bar itself. It may not have been the first nougat bar to sell itself on sheer longevity of the chewing experience (several children who purchased the short-lived Cadbury's Big One in 1971 are still finishing it today as they leaf through their unit trust portfolios), but the combination of that star-spangled wrapper and a block booking of ad breaks on *Tiswas* enticed a generation to 'bite through the chocolate and chew... real slow'. Just don't mention the suffocating tedium.

*TOBLERONE

You know you're talking about continental chocolate when you have to censor its origins for the under-twelves. Get your Toblerone history from *Blue Peter*, and they'd tell you a quaint tale of Swiss chocolatier Theodor Tobler being inspired to shape his new nougat, honey and almond-laced creation by rugged Alpine scenery. Ask someone closer

Opposite: Toblerone (1908). Considerably more successful than Toblertwo or Toblerthree.

Below: Love triangle. A soft-focus effect for Suchard's 1982 product catalogue.

95

to Tobler, and you'll get a less edifying yarn about the old man getting so turned on by a pyramid of derriére-thrusting dancers at the Folies Bergères he recreates the memorable pile of women's arses using the brown stuff. Depends what you go for in a story, really.

Granite or gluteous, the saw-toothed prism shape set the Toblerone apart from other chocolate bars, most of which didn't get to travel about in a special snug-fitting box. In Britain, though, it had additional cachet. Possession of any of the bar's bigger sizes (and, boy, did they get massive, up to a whopping ten-kilo edition) meant one thing: check out the flash git who's been abroad. Though not strictly foreign fare – Crosse & Blackwell had the licence to make them in their Newham factory from 1929 onwards – it was seen seldom enough, and never in such gigantic dimensions, that it became a totem for the well-travelled child of the world.

Fine for junior showboating, not so good for UK sales. To get the bar out of the duty free and into supermarkets, the boys from Suchard spent potloads. Televisual whimsy about triangular bees providing the honey surfaced in 1984. White chocolate came in 1985, and an affordable 18p snack size in 1986. The Toblerone slowly adapted itself to the unforgiving British climate. Then Suchard

went too far: they tried to buy out Rowntree, losing to those other mountainous Swiss chocolatiers, Nestlé. Moral: the British are up for new ideas, but don't push your luck. Especially if your flagship product provides the most uncomfortable eating experience in the Western hemisphere.

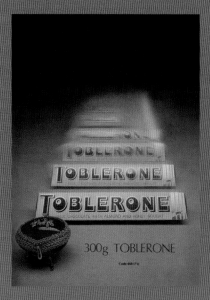
300g TOBLERONE

*TOFFO

That old-timery 'o' on the end betrays the pre-war origins of Mackintosh's venerable roll of 'Toff-O-Luxe super crème toffees', but after several decades of unfussy plain flavouring, those squat little cylinders which pleasingly moulded themselves to the creases of their individual wrappers underwent a bit of a renaissance. Or they were

Opposite: Toffo (1939), the earliest recorded instance of 'checking what colour the next one is before offering them round' behaviour.

Below: There's a new deputy in town. Mackintosh recruits a toffee posse, circa 1976.

97

endlessly mucked about with, depending on your level of curmudgeonly attachment to confectionery tradition.

After a brief and ill-fated dabbling with a patently all wrong blackcurrant variant (doubtless an attempt to replicate the soaraway success of their Fruit Pastilles 'tube with all black ones'), mint and a sophisticated rum and butter flavour joined the originals on the shelves in 1971. But they struck the mother lode five years later with the dark blue assorted roll, wherein old plainy was joined by the instantly popular chocolate flavour, the rather less popular strawberry, and the obligatory pariah flavour, banana with a distinctly chemical tang. As with all variety packs, consumers endlessly complained of a perceived lack of the first of these, and a malicious overabundance of the last.

Perhaps to help police the discontent, TV ads introduced the Toffo sheriff, a super-cool sharpshooter who effortlessly picked absconding bank robbers off a rope bridge without getting up from his lazily tilted chair. 'Go get 'em, Floyd,' he drawled to his wet-behind-the-ears deputy, while the voice-over mused, 'A man's gotta chew what a man's gotta chew,' seemingly oblivious to the brand confusion it was sowing

in young viewers' tiny minds by drawing itself uncomfortably close to its rival in Midwest-themed mastication, the Texan Bar.

It held its own, though, surviving into the '80s when, in an outbreak of madness at executive level, the sainted chocolate flavour was replaced with... blackcurrant! Another warning from history unheeded, another queasy aftertaste to choke unhappily down. When will people learn?

*TURKISH DELIGHT

Hardly extinct and, at any rate, never really a candidate for that impulsive tuck shop purchase, Fry's Turkish Delight is nevertheless inherently nostalgic. Bristol-based apothecary Joseph Fry began churning out slabs nearly 100 years ago at his Small Street premises, yet it lingers on shelves like an almost shameful secret to this day. Indeed, Cadbury seems to have forgotten that it makes the bar, which still bears the Fry name and a packet design that hasn't changed in five decades. The recipe remains a classic Anglicised version of *lokum* (boiled sugar syrup simmered with starch and cream of tartar), the likes of which would turn up at Christmas in suspiciously hexagonal boxes jam-packed with icing sugar and gooey, gummy, rose-flavoured lumps of unknown origin. Fry's chocolate-coated variety took many forms before settling on the now familiar block, roughly the size, shape and texture of a human tongue, for the more discriminating Anglo-Saxon palate.

Though historically associated with temptation (via Narnia's White Witch), Turkish Delight was invariably the Friday night treat of choice for any mum in search of what the industry deemed 'a slow, savoured eat' and the chance to put her feet up after a day's slaving. (Her personal ottoman empire was just that back bedroom storage divan for spare blankets and bedding.) The name itself hinted at the kind of carnal pleasures one might only experience in the non-Christian East – what Alan Whicker called the 'mosques, minarets and mayhem' of Istanbul (not Constantinople) on behalf of Barclaycard – and which Cadbury more than happily alluded to

from the 1950s onwards in a series of television ads 'full of Eastern promise' (whatever that is). A succession of mysterious, raven-haired beauties reclined to receive the attentions of brooding, dark-skinned Bedouin men on horseback, though the desert scenes often owed more to Acton than Ankara. This was an era when belly dancers were thought the very height of exotic sophistication, and the merest hint of a pierced navel would send men giddy with desire.

In 1981, however, Cadbury dispensed with any attempt at realism and commissioned 'Shifting Sands', a lavish, eerily lit montage of vaguely Middle Eastern imagery, featuring a snake, Saudi sand dunes and the dulcet tones of Anthony Valentine over Cliff Adams's haunting pan-pipe soundtrack. As other companies found out to their cost (whither the Tobler Turkish, for example?), the product was peculiarly sensitive to advertising, and so Cadbury took a scimitar to the Turkish Delight budget, slashing it Gordian-knot style. In the thirty years since, not a penny has been spent on updating the campaign. Thus it remains, languishing at the very back of their back catalogue, a mirage-like reminder of an altogether more indulgent age.

*TWIX

We humans are an essentially primitive species. Our flabby, wasteful brain is easily fooled. This is about the level of neuroscientific knowledge required to work in a chocolate factory. Start pointing and naming things like the amygdala and you're probably overqualified. But arrange your chocolate bars like

Opposite: Twix of the trade. Mars's two-fingered salute to the competition (1967).

Below: The dawn of the designer ice cream. *Baywatch* bunkum and binoculars in a Twix campaign circa 1993.

101

schoolchildren in a newsagent's, two at a time, and the keys to the kingdom will be yours.

Mars was most successful at foxing our equivocal minds with the introduction in 1967 of the Twix, a heady double cocktail of chocolate, caramel and shortcake biscuit, surely the most inoffensive of ingredients. But if it's a biscuit, then what's it doing here? According to the VAT-man, it's not a biscuit, which means it can't be taxed as a luxury item. But it's not entirely a chocolate bar either. It can only be described as a confection, decided Mars; a law unto itself; a snack.

Hence the unusual name, so called not only because of its twin-bar nature, but also because it occupies a no-man's-land 'twixt biscuit and bar. Initially, it was marketed with a 'longer lasting' promise, although that could easily be misinterpreted as a thumbing of the nose to sell-by dates. Then, as if genuinely trying to flaunt its tax-exile status, Twix tried to insert itself into that bastion of biscuit consumption, the Great British tea break. Traditional nibbles were mocked at every turn. Innuendo abounded. The window cleaner couldn't drop by an open window without offering to share a finger with the secretary. Girls couldn't meet their fella in the park without giving him one. It was like the Robin Askwith 'Confessions' films re-edited for the under-eights.

Ironically, these scenes were almost exclusively populated by soon-to-be-stars of children's television. Jobbing actors they may have been but, look, there's that girl from *Hickory House*. And isn't that the ponce off *The Tomorrow People*? And her from *Blue Peter* with the pop star daughter? Indeed, like a pregnant Janet Ellis, Twix just kept getting bigger through the '80s, gaining extra length and an additional ten grams in 1984 to keep up with some of its arch-rivals, Rowntree's Drifter, and Cadbury's Time Out and Twirl among them.

By this time, even Twix had stopped going on about its superior binary qualities, preferring instead to rattle on about abstract ideas like the 'snack gap' and its suitability to fit therein. Accordingly, our primitive brains had wised up and were no longer taken in by the twin-pack trick. It was, sadly, now just our waistlines that had grown flabby.

*VIMTO LOLLY

Who loves ya, baby? TV's Lieutenant Kojak, that's who – not the only famous lollipop licker of the 1970s, but probably the baldest. The show's writers decided to give the hard-bitten New York detective his trademark Tootsie Pop in a move to appease the anti-smoking brigade. His favourite flavour? Low tar.

Opposite: Yes, yes, 'Vimto' is an anagram of 'vomit'. But 'Vimto Lollies' is an anagram of... er... 'Moi loves Lilt.' Vimto lollies circa 1977.

103

If the sweet makers had their way, though, every telly star from Weatherfield to Walmington-on-Sea would have had a lollipop stick protruding from between their lips. Or any other orifice, for that matter. Big-name backing was a good way to steal a march on the competition. Lollies had been commonplace since the eighteenth century – namechecked in works by Thackeray and Coleridge, no less – so what better way to differentiate than to slap on a celebrity seal of approval?

Liverpool-based Tavener and Rutledge landed a significant number of exclusive deals for the UK, bagging the big screen *Batman* and *Bugsy Malone* for a string of signature lollies, as well as Telly Savalas himself for the obligatory *Kojak* tie-in. Eric 'n' Ernie brought strawberries and cream-shaped sunshine on a stick, while Laurel and Hardy, experiencing an inexplicable mid-1970s revival, also shared the same flavours for Ollie's Lollies. Blue Bird plumped for another Saturday night light entertainment staple and launched the *It's A Knockout* gobstopper lolly in 1979, though this was quickly eclipsed by 3p Buck Rogers pops – available in five flavours: cosmic traffic light, galactic lemon fizz, terrestrial treacle, draconian lime and meteorite melon.

However, for flavour, and sheer why-didn't-I-think-of-that-first

chutzpah, the Vimto lolly outshone them all. Patriotic in a red, white and blue livery, echoing the traditional striped awnings of Olde English market stalls, Vimto was the very model of balance between modernity and nostalgia. Run up on Swizzels Matlow's state-of-the-art lolly-making machinery, yet with a taste reminiscent of Sunday evenings round at Grandma's house, it was that Holy Grail of the confectionery crusades: an instant classic.

And it was almost immediately superseded. The days of one lolly, one flavour ended abruptly with the arrival of Chupa Chups. Literally translated as 'sucky suck', these whorish lollies burst into the UK market like refugees from a Catalonian hen night on the Costa Brava. Flaunting all kinds of exotic, foreign flavours, and a garish Salvador Dalí-designed logo, they spoke nothing of the past and looked set to trample all over the future.

Marketing is all. Those lollipop men would have more luck hooking up with today's selection of big-headed, stick-thin-bodied celebrities for a bit of cross-promotional candy action. As for Chupa Chups' recent 'stop smoking, start sucking' slogan? Well, at least Kojak would have approved.

plain chocolate
vanilla flavour

ROWNTREE'S
walnut
whip

*WALNUT WHIP

Around since time immemorial but reinvented for a new, late '60s generation by Rowntree (they immediately removed the interior walnut and have since stealthily upped the outer-gloss factor on the chocolate body), the Walnut Whip is deeply ingrained in popular snack culture. Perhaps not a delicacy to be purchased on a whim – for

Opposite: One Walnut Whip (1910). The exact cost per London resident of the Olympic Games 2012, according to Ken Livingstone. Remember him?

Below: What's the betting this was pitched 105 as 'a kind of Alice In Walnutland' by the ad agency? Lose yourself in impenetrable symbolism, circa 1986.

who would want a Walnut Whim anyway? – it was something that had to be carefully planned for. Newsagents could only stack them in boxes of three, thanks to the unusual beacon shape, square cardboard footprint and unhelpful cellophane wrapping, so they would seldom be seen in the house other than on special occasions.

To be frank, associations with highly polished Jaguar dashboards, strange pickle jars at the back of a grandparent's pantry, and that *Fawlty Towers* Waldorf salad episode already lent anything walnutty an air of specialness. Dads, typically cracking their way through a Christmas Eve bowl of nuts, would often be called upon to dispose of that top-mounted kernel (an acquired taste by anyone's standards), so that the remaining foam fondant funnel could be devoured unsullied. The altogether less innocent act of licking out the cream was wilfully transplanted by Ann Summers party organisers into their repertoire of saucy fun 'n' games, the cheeky monkeys.

Television advertisers, however, struggled to convey the Walnut Whip's unique appeal. A '70s attempt at volcano-centric, cloud-swirling psychedelia was supplanted by bizarre, office-based 'most fun you can have on your own' farce, before the usual chocolate ad fluff of whirling skirts,

spiral staircases and a wistful Pan's Labyrinth montage took over in the '80s. Ultimately, immortality was ensured not by absorption into Cockney rhyming slang (it apparently translates as either 'acid trip', 'the snip' or 'kip', which must make conversation dahn the Auld Bull and Bush a constant challenge), nor as a literary simile for anything roughly conical in cheap novels ('60s women's hairstyles, Madonna's brassieres, or men's doo-dahs), but by a name-check in the 2002 top ten hit, 'What's Your Flava'. Because you know when you've made Craig David 'sick to the point of throwing up' you're at the top of your game.

*WHAM

Playing the home advantage only gets you so far. For the best part of the twentieth century, Stenhousemuir-based toffee merchants McCowan's chugged along just fine with their none-more-traditional Highland Toffee, save a brief surfing of the Zeitgeist in the form of 1975's Brent-tastic Oil Rig Toffee. All this sporran-tossing homeliness was overshadowed in 1980, however, with the wide-eyed announcement of 'McCowan's first venture into the space age!'. Woo! The space age had practically ended by this point, but never mind, what exactly was the deal? Only 'the fruity, chewy space age bar that sizzles with sherbet!'. That's what!

Yes, out went meek old brown toffee, and in came the lurid, tangy pink of the tooth-rotting Wham bar, with a tingle on the tongue, a rocket on the wrapper and, indeed, a ker-ching in the tills. An astronomical 2 million 10p bars and utterly out of this world 40 million 2p chews were sold in 1982, possibly because Wham had something for everyone. Adventurous kids got off on the chemical fizz and dental danger. Those of a scientific bent pondered on the way it could warp, like space and time, into an infinitely long raspberry superhighway, where the very laws of confectionery break down. Sci-fi nuts, meanwhile, could get off on the adventures of the good ship *Wham*, as chronicled in a series of 'amusing-dramatic' radio ads.

Matters took an unusual twist in 1983 with the arrival of the Zegazoid, 'the frightening new liquorice and lime chew bar'. Bedecked with green-bonced aliens, who somehow engaged the Wham bar in 'a mid-space struggle for power', the new chew was soon sent packing, despite undercutting

its foe by 5p a throw. However, some also remember Gorgo, 'a green monster from the planet Gorg', who lent his name to an alternative version, 'a cosmic green chew bar with fizzy fruit flavour'. Was this the work of a parallel continuum? Or McCowan's hedging their bets? Given that, for either bar, the name 'Gangrene' was seriously considered, it's probably best not to second-guess the motive.

Back on earth, McCowan's struggled to meet that 'difficult second album' challenge. Mumbo Gumbo was a tropical fruit flavoured chew with a fey hippo for a mascot. Dennis the Menace borrowed the *Beano*'s scowling scallywag wholesale for a red and black striped raspberry and blackcurrant bar. Most inevitably, however, an alliance with Barr's Irn-Bru took regional loyalty to its natural conclusion. In 1989 a management buy-out from Nestlé returned the company to Scottish hands, and ambitions once again turned to the stars. Unfortunately, McCowan's chewy cherry cola MASK tie-in was yet another dud, but Wham kept the mission ticking over long after the last Saturn V rocket had gone the way of those juvenile choppers.

*WISPA

I t's a lazy journalist's dream: a chocolate bar from the 1980s that was a triumph of marketing over substance. The Wispa's Aero-meets-Flake texture didn't exactly spark a confectionery revolution when the fluffy ingot made its debut in the Tyne Tees area. What raised eyebrows were the TV ads: wry chunks of two-handed banter between

famous celebs of the day. Even
so, it wasn't a Zeitgeist-surfing
triumph from the off. Picking
the stars of *Dad's Army* and *The
Sweeney* was an odd gambit
in the days before retro chic
turned every old brown sitcom
into a nostalgic goldmine, while
the choice of the third show,
Shoestring, was just plain weird.
A shabby regional detective with
mental health issues – he'll tell
us what to eat, right, kids? By
the time of the bar's nationwide
roll-out two years later, they'd
perfected a more contemporary
line-up: *It Ain't Half Hot Mum* and
Yes, Minister may not have been
trendy, but they were at least
current, and the *Hi-De-Hi* ad, with
Ruth Madoc and Simon Cadell in
full sexually charged character,
but cannily using each other's
real names to avoid legal
hassles, tapped a rich seam
of chocoroticism mined
further by Paul Nicholas and
Jan Francis, and real-life
bedfellows Rula Lenska and
Dennis Waterman, set off by
the nudge-nudge strapline 'Bite
it and believe it'.

By the end of the decade,
Cadbury were packing the
edgier likes of Peter Cook
and Mel Smith off to ramble
in front of a black cloth at
Shepperton Studios, under
the banner 'You're thinking
chocolate, you're talking Wispa',
while Noel Edmonds, rather
worryingly, demanded, 'Know

someone who just has to keep
doing it?' While all this was going
on, the brand diversified into
the sickly Wispa Gold, the Wispa
Mint and the biscuity Wispa Bite.
This expansionism proved a bit
much, as sales declined through
the '90s, until all varieties were
discontinued in 2003. But you can't
keep a good marketing man down,
and within a few years Cadbury,
overwhelmed by 'grassroots
public demand', reinstated the
bar following a suspiciously well-
orchestrated Internet
campaign. This is
what's known
in the trade
as 'doing an
Arctic Roll'.

*YORKIE

There comes a time in every sweet-toothed boy's life when he takes a look at the contents of the paper bag he's just blown his hard-pestered 50p on, and finds it lacking... something. Maybe it's the colour (all those pink shrimps), maybe it's the texture (soft, as a rule), but something about the whole affair suddenly seems a bit, well, wet.

Opposite: If you don't like trucking, tough luck! Plenty of choice for the school hard-case courtesy of Yorkie (1976).

Below: Wagon wheels! A Yorkie Easter egg, circa 1982.

111

There are, of course, sweets to help you look a bit 'hard'. You could stock up on the bracing Army & Navy Mints – if you don't mind pulling faces all afternoon. You could pretend to tug on a chocolate Woodbine or ponce about with a liquorice pipe like a Fisher-Price Tony Benn, but not even the junior kids are fooled by that kind of carry-on. No, there's only one truly manly item of confectionery on the sweet shop shelves – the Yorkie bar.

This was a bit of marketing genius on the part of Rowntree employee (and later CEO of EMI), Eric Nicoli. Cadbury had let their main asset, the Dairy Milk, fall into a state of disrepair in the '70s. Rowntree saw their moment, and dived in with a bar of such unprecedented solidity that the word 'chunky' just wouldn't do it justice. The Yorkie mythology was stoked by an ad campaign harking back to their ancient Motoring Chocolate brand, wherein a Kwik Save Johnny Cash sang a driving country paean to the macho sweetmeat: 'Good, rich and thick/A milk chocolate brick.' On the screen a hard-bitten long-distance lorry driver hauled his Scammel across rugged terrain with only his trusty Yorkie bar for company (a pretty sad state of affairs in retrospect, but for a pre-pubescent boy a man at the wheel of anything bigger

than a Datsun Cherry is little short of a god).

Most important of all, the Yorkie was the centre of possibly the only male initiation rite to involve emulsified cocoa butter. The ability to take a Yorkie straight from the fridge and bite off a chunk with a satisfying snap, and without leaving any fragments of teeth in the remaining bar, was as sure a sign of maturity as the ability to do press-ups or claim you'd copped off with Nadine Jones without inviting a dozen spontaneous impressions of Jimmy Hill. If you can eat a Yorkie without wincing, you'll be a man, my son.

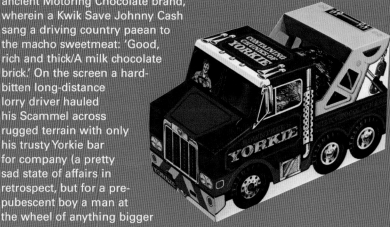

Acknowledgements

Louis Barfe, Andy Blackford, Norton Canes, Paul Dennis, Sarah-Louise Heslop, Roger McKechnie, Rob McKoen, James Nichols, Jon Peake, Nicholas Pegg, Whitby Specialist Vehicles Limited.

Thanks

Rachel Faulkner, Luana Gobbo, Corinna Harrod, Scott Pack, Liam Relph, Clarissa San Pedro.